HOW MANY
MILES TO BABYLON?

Also by Adewale Maja-Pearce

Loyalties and Other Stories
In My Father's Country

How Many
Miles to Babylon?

An essay

ADEWALE MAJA-PEARCE

HEINEMANN : LONDON

To my mother,
and to the memory
of my grandparents

I would like to thank the Society of Authors
for the grant that helped me write this book.
And thanks to Monty Courage,
who got the car on the road.

William Heinemann Ltd
Michelin House, 81 Fulham Road, London SW3 6RB
LONDON   MELBOURNE   AUCKLAND

First published 1990
Copyright © Adewale Maja-Pearce 1990

A CIP catalogue record for this book
is available from the British Library
ISBN 0 434 44172 4

Extracts from the *Salisbury Review* and
the *Star* are reprinted with their permission.
The author thanks Faber and Faber for
granting permission to quote
from Derek Walcott's *Midsummer* sequence.

Typeset by Deltatype Limited, Ellesmere Port
Printed in Great Britain by
St Edmundsbury Press Ltd, Bury St Edmunds, Suffolk

How many miles to Babylon?
Three score and ten.
Can I get there by candle light?
Yes, and back again.

1

Dave's place

Winds of the World, give answer! They are
   Whimpering to and fro –
And what should they know of England who only
   England know?

Rudyard Kipling: 'The English Flag'

When I arrived back from Canada with the manuscript of my first novel I rented a room in Notting Hill Gate. It was a small room with a sink in one corner, a single bed in another, and one of those cheap, vinyl-covered tables that fold down at either end. The walls were painted a mustard yellow, although somebody had begun to apply a coat of purple to break the monotony. They hadn't gone further than the top half of one wall. So it remained for the nine months that I lived there; so it probably remains today.

London is full of such rooms. In that house there were sixteen of them, all occupied by transients of one sort or another, by foreigners washed up in a more stable society but who had no other connection with the country they were living in than the four walls they inhabited and perhaps, if they were lucky, a job as dishwasher or hotel porter or Underground guard. We rarely spoke to one another. Sometimes we met on the stairs but otherwise we kept to ourselves. A quick nod of recognition was the most that passed between us, as if anything more intimate might lead to unwelcome complications.

The only time one of them spoke to me was when a thief broke into the house and went methodically through every room. I had gone to Swansea for the week-end to see some friends from my university days. Before I left I took my typewriter to my brother's for safekeeping, as if I knew in advance what was going to happen. All I lost was a cheap camera I had never used; but the knowledge that someone I didn't know had been in the room and rifled through my belongings made me feel that the room was no longer mine, as if I now shared it with a stranger whose intentions towards me were purely malevolent. There was never any question of calling the police. People who lived like us were shy of the authorities, some no doubt for good reason.

That was in the winter and spring of 1976/77. Every afternoon, when I woke up, I would sit at the table and work on a short story on the big electric typewriter that I had carted across the Atlantic. I wrote the stories at the rate of two or three a week and entered them for every competition I came across. In the meantime, I had sent the manuscript of my novel to a publishing house and was waiting for their reply. I don't remember doubting that the novel would be accepted. It was only much later, when I began to understand something about the nature of creativity, that I realised how dreadful my manuscript really was. The short stories I was writing were hardly any better; but as with the novel, which I wrote in six months flat, I had no means of judging them. I was too ignorant and in any case my motives were suspect. Looking back I can see that I had an idea of literature as a means of self-promotion, which is the worst possible reason for wanting to write.

I was also confused. This was hardly surprising. My real subject – who I was and where I belonged – was far too vague. I wanted certainties; I wanted a fixed place in the universe. My life was too fragmented. Coping with the emotional consequences of that fragmentation on a day-to-day level was exhausting enough. I didn't possess the energy or the resources to explore my predicament, and even if I had I wouldn't have known how to go about it. At that stage I was still trying to discover what kind of writer I was. It took me a long time to find out that I had little or no talent for fiction, and longer again to understand the possibilities of the essay as a viable form for saying what I wanted to say.

Day after day I sat at the vinyl table in that purple-and-mustard room filling reams of paper with lies and fabrications and trying to impose order where there was none. I was using literature to create the order that I conspicuously lacked. I only wonder that I stuck at it, a combination perhaps of stubbornness and lack of choice. I had backed myself into a corner by giving up on my M.A., the ostensible reason for going to Canada, within the first three months of arriving. The immediate catalyst for this dramatic change of direction was an attack of flu over the Christmas vacation and a fortnight in bed reading the collected works of Henry Miller.

Miller is not a great writer, but between my heightened state and his intoxicating talk of personal liberation I found the courage to admit what I had hidden from myself in my pursuit of what I had mistakenly assumed to be security and stability. It hadn't been necessary to travel as far as Canada to discover that I had no stomach for academia, for those fat volumes with long footnotes which were waiting for me on my desk and which I knew I would never bring myself to read; but it helped that Canada was, for me, a neutral country towards which I had no emotional ties.

A few days after I had made my decision to quit the university I met a man who worked for the local branch of Olivetti. When I told him what I had done he gave me, gratis, a reconditioned office typewriter, a beautiful machine and far more expensive than any I could have afforded. If ever a sign were needed this was it. Naturally I saw the hand of God in the welcome gift since I have never believed in coincidence. There is a pattern to these things, which in turn are the clues to our destiny. So I became a writer and wrote the manuscript that I brought back with me to London.

In fact the M.A. was to have been my passport to Nigeria, my father's country, where, with my father's help, I could so easily have fallen into a teaching job in one of the many new universities which were built on the proceeds of the sudden oil wealth. 'Our problem is not money but how to spend it,' the then Nigerian Head of State declared shortly before he was toppled from power. I could have returned to Nigeria and collected my share of this bonanza, but even as I played around with this seductive fantasy I knew that it wasn't a possibility. I was British, not Nigerian; and it was to Britain that I returned, to that purple-and-mustard attic room in Notting Hill Gate.

I suppose there was also a measure of perversity in my fantasies of returning to Nigeria, and this apart from the genuine and profound connection with a country in which I had spent a large part of my childhood. One always imagines that one's life will be better elsewhere: between the ages of twelve and sixteen I had dreamed of nothing but returning to Britain, where I was born and where I had lived with my grandparents for a year when I was eleven; when I finally did make it over here, in 1970, I thought continuously of returning to Nigeria. Thirteen years were to pass before I stepped on Nigerian soil again. Ironically, it was only by going back to Nigeria that I learnt to understand – and appreciate – many things about Britain which I hadn't been able to see before.

I mean 'see' in the literal sense: not quite the universe

in a grain of sand, perhaps, but to see the landscape and the autumn colours and the quality of the light; and to see all these as belonging to a discrete place which is different from any other place.

The ability to see is not a given; it is something we have to learn. This is especially true of the obvious, everyday objects by which we are surrounded and which for that reason we so easily overlook: the style of architecture of a specific period; a species of bird at a certain time of year; a common flower repeated in any number of front gardens. These are the otherwise insignificant details which finally distinguish a society from any other at the same time as they invest that society with depth and resonance.

In our tourist age, with cheap travel and package holidays, we are encouraged to look at what isn't obvious and everyday so that we come to associate a place only with the fabulous: Kenya is wildlife; China is the Forbidden City; England is Salisbury Cathedral and the Tower of London. But all these are unique and therefore demand our attention. In the process we will miss everything in between; we will overlook what is commonplace.

Seeing begins with naming. We can only be said to properly see what we can name because it is only language which has the power to make the world real: 'In the beginning was the Word, and the Word was with God, and the Word was God.' But the tourist brochures which give us the history of the Cathedral and the list of those beheaded in the Tower don't make it their business to tell us the names of the shrubs around either monument, though we might very well register, but distantly, the figure of the gardener raking the autumn leaves.

I have only recently begun to see trees. The first tree I

saw was the copper beech when a friend of mine, an Englishman with a strong West Country accent and a deep love for his country – the passionate, unspoken love which the British have for their country and which isn't to be confused with vulgar nationalism – pointed one out to me and called it by its name. It was a particularly splendid specimen in the middle of a small park in Swansea. I had walked through this park sometimes twice a day for three or more years, but for the first time since I had been in Britain I looked at a copper beech.

This was progress indeed: it had taken all of seven years for me to make such a simple discovery. From then on, whenever I went for a walk, I would search out copper beeches. And gradually, over a period of time, I began to learn the names of other trees. Every tree that I could give a name to became distinctive, individual, itself: oak, elm, birch; fine, strong English names, fine and strong like the language itself. I now have a vocabulary of half a dozen, a modest number no doubt to those with a deeper connection with the country and everything that it contains, but for sentimental reasons the copper beech remains my favourite.

When I came to Britain at sixteen, on the verge of adulthood, I couldn't name any trees. For that reason all trees looked the same; all trees *were* the same. Every tree was just a tree and no different from any other tree anywhere. So it was with everything else. I was like a person with defective vision who saw only the hazy outlines of the surrounding world. And instead of trying to look, instead of learning the names of the objects around me, I retreated into the fantasy of life in another place. But it was a childish fantasy, and childish not in the literal sense that Nigeria was the place of my childhood, but because if I couldn't learn to look in

Britain there was no reason to suppose I would be able to look in Nigeria.

It was V. S. Naipaul who once said, in an essay published in 1958, that he could never write about Britain: '. . . I feel I know so little about England. I have met many people but I know them only in official attitudes – the drink, the interview, the meal. I have a few friends. But this gives me only a superficial knowledge of the country, and in order to write fiction it is necessary to know so much . . .'

He wrote this after he had been here only a short while. Thirty years later he published a book, *The Enigma of Arrival*, about a writer from Trinidad of Indian descent who came to Britain at the age of eighteen and thirty years later is living in a cottage in the heart of the English countryside. The writer takes a daily stroll in the garden, which is part of the estate on which he is living; and the garden then becomes a symbol of the writer's quest: 'His garden taught me about the seasons, and I got to know in a new way things I must have seen many times before. I saw the blossom come out on his well-pruned apple trees, got to know the colour of the blossom . . .'

The Enigma of Arrival is a meditation on seeing: it is only through 'seeing' the English garden that the writer arrives at a sense of home; previously, 'I saw what I saw very clearly. But I didn't know what I was looking at. I had nothing to fit it into. I was still in a kind of limbo.' That was it precisely; that was the predicament of the immigrant, the outsider, the stranger in a new land. I was surprised at the extent to which the British reviewers missed the courage of Naipaul's achievement, the homage he had paid to their country in adopting it as his own, but Naipaul has become an unfashionable writer.

When I had lived in Nigeria and thought only of going to Britain I was equally impervious to everything around me. I couldn't even speak the language of the place, the language which described and gave reality to the physical universe I so casually inhabited. The fantasy had nothing to do with the real world, and it was seductive to the extent that it relieved me of the necessity of engaging with the here and now, with the world as it exists independently of our desires, or what we take to be our desires. And I have only recently begun to understand that my partial vision was a comment on the fragility of my own sense of identity. I could only cope with the world by reducing it to manageable portions, like the packaged cheese one buys in the supermarket: bland, but easy to spread. The less I had to take on board the simpler it was for me to function.

If I had completed my M.A. and gone back to Nigeria I would have merely been running away from the necessity of engaging with the world. Nigeria, Britain, Canada, back to Nigeria: each time I was challenged to look my response would have been to flee. I had even, briefly, played with the idea of going to South America when I had to leave Canada and I was beginning to panic in the way only the insecure can, with that underlying hysteria. To that end I had written to the various embassies asking for details of their visa requirements. Why South America? Why not? It was flight for its own sake, flight to another landscape, another language, until the novelty wore off and then flight again just at the moment when a deeper engagement was demanded.

Many people live like this. They aren't to be envied.

Such a life is shallow, and the shallowness is made tackier by the supposed glamour of airports and visas and a certain knowingness: how to handle immigration officials; how to haggle with taxi drivers; how to find the non-tourist bars within twenty-four hours. The tourists themselves, from whom one is desperately trying to dissociate oneself, then become objects of ridicule and scorn precisely because one is lumped with them in the eyes of the native for whom one foreigner is much like any other. And always one is living on the edge of society. Your presence doesn't matter to the native, except perhaps as an irritant as you loudly proclaim your credentials and push up the prices of local goods.

The other day I met an Australian in a pub in Earls Court, as one is always meeting Australians in pubs in Earls Court. Within fifteen minutes he had mentioned Bangkok, Delhi, Alexandria, Rio. He had been in London for six months but already he was thinking of moving on. Where to? He shrugged, and then reeled off another list. But they were just exotic, 'Third World' places, names in an atlas one might have been leafing through in front of the fire on a wet November evening and suggesting only fantasy: cheap drugs, cheap whores, cheap lives; the fantasy of experience for its own sake made possible by your possession of a currency which can buy anything under the sun, including human beings.

This Australian knew nothing of London, never mind Britain; and I could see, as he talked, how little he observed his immediate surroundings. He didn't even see the person to whom he was talking. He was only concerned to establish his reality, as if he were in imminent danger of disintegrating unless he could continually validate himself in the fleeting conscious-ness of a complete stranger. He didn't connect; he belonged nowhere; he formed no part of the consciousness of a specific community in a specific place on the earth, which is largely how we have our being. That he had been born in Australia was only a matter of chance; that he was presently drinking in a pub in London was equally accidental. He didn't stand on the earth, which is why he was happiest when he was airborne. Later, as we sat in his confined room in one of the anonymous hotels nearby and he started talking about the way he made his money and his narrow escapes (but he'll be caught one day and sent to prison), I noticed a British Airways timetable on the floor beside his single bed. This was his bedtime reading.

Any life seems better than this, including the materially impoverished existence of a peasant scraping the soil of his native place. The peasant touches every plant he coaxes to the surface; is familiar with the sky as it prepares to let down the rains; fashions with the soles of his feet the path between hut and field. He sees his universe and is part of it; he connects with the earth; he has a wholeness denied the Australian in Earls Court. For this reason he would see more in that pub than the Australian, more than the Australian would ever see. I aspired to that wholeness, even as I knew that my own seeing could only ever be an approximation, a determined intellectual exercise dependent on the will to achieve what should ideally be instinctive.

I had to learn as best I could to be at home, but even the word 'home' had complex connotations. Where was home? Was it Nigeria, my father's country? Or was it Britain, my mother's country? And how far did allegiance to the one involve a betrayal of the other? My inability to see was inseparable from the sense of betrayal. If I didn't look, if I didn't admit the reality of the particular corner of the world in which I happened to be, in this case Britain – 'This blessed plot, this earth, this realm, this England' – then I couldn't be said to properly live here. This in turn meant that I was released from the necessity of confronting the nature of my allegiance because to admit Britain, to say that I was British and have done with it, was to deny Nigeria. I was like a man married to one woman but trying to remain faithful to another. If I wasn't careful I would lose both, and in the end I would be the one to suffer for it: to live like this is to condemn oneself to a half-life, which is the predicament of the outsider.

The outsider, the person who is fated to live perpetually on the margins of society, has been invested with a certain romance, so much so that the word itself has become one of those words which we use without thinking about what it means in actual, human terms, in terms of real people who live in the real world. There is nothing the least romantic in such a destiny; and to the extent that I share something of the condition of the outsider, I am appalled by my own sense of fragmentation.

When I came over at sixteen I was friendly with Winston. He was Jamaican but had lived here most of his life. Jamaica was only a dim recollection – mango trees and blue ocean – but in all the time I knew him he spoke continually of returning to the West Indies, of going 'home'. He did so in much the same way that I spoke of returning to Nigeria. It was our shared but unspoken sense of alienation which drew us together, and I think I half-consciously understood his forced nostalgia as part of his survival mechanism.

Everything about his life suggested impermanence, from the temporary jobs he took up and discarded with unthinking ease on the same trading estate in Wembley where I worked (those were the days of full employment when you could walk into the Labour Exchange on Friday and start work on Monday), to the hideous room he rented from an aunt I never met. Those London rooms again: the yellowing paint around the window frames; the drab second-hand furniture; the formica table that folded down at either end. His room was no more than a convenience between work and pub and a place to sleep at the end of the day. It was not home in any recognisable sense.

Winston and I quickly fell into a routine of meeting at week-ends and wandering about rather aimlessly. We never had enough money to do anything sensible. In the course of the evening we would invariably end up at the indoor bowling alley just off the High Street. He always had high hopes of meeting women there. The only women we ever met were two sisters who told us that they lived in Hemel Hempstead. I didn't then know where Hemel Hempstead was, and when I asked Winston he curled his lip in such a way as to suggest that it was as near the end of the earth as made little difference. In any event he didn't consider it worth our while pursuing the matter, a fact which impressed me even more than the curled lip.

Sometimes we would go to a Blues party. This was before they became the fashionable expression of authentic West Indian culture, culture being defined so widely as to become a department of anthropology: any expression of difference will do, and who are we to judge its relative merits? Apart from the fact that I couldn't abide reggae, I disliked the atmosphere at these parties. Fights were forever breaking out over women or drugs or both, and there was a perpetual undercurrent of racial tension: a white woman who didn't accept the

14

advances of a black man – any black man – was branded a racist; a white man who came with a black woman – but this was rare – was continually put on his guard. I thought it was all a despicable and futile game played by men who had accepted their marginalisation in society and were now seizing the opportunity to exploit the little power they were able to exercise in the fragile protectorate they occupied for the night: fragile because the police could break up these gatherings any time they felt like it; fragile because, in the morning, bleary-eyed and hung-over, nothing would have changed.

Why did I react so strongly? Because I could have submitted to the same; because I could have sought identity in terms of colour. The race issue, so called, was only then beginning to impinge on me; and it would have been easy, given my confused emotional state at the time, to have found sanctuary in colour. But I knew instinctively that it wasn't a real option for me – for anybody, come to that – and I had my Nigerian inheritance to thank for that knowledge. Nigerian society is exclusive. Every Nigerian is the inheritor of a powerful tradition. These traditions easily transcended the encounter with Europe, which in any case encompassed the life of one generation. The fact of survival ultimately strengthened the sense of self. The Nigerian, like the Briton, knows very well who they are. Whatever angst the Nigerian intellectual suffers in relation to Europe is being worked out at a deeper level than that of mere colour.

If nothing else my inheritance had taught me that colour was not among the attributes of human beings in any sense which mattered. I already saw too far beyond the constrictions of so shallow an idea of humanity. But I was fortunate, certainly more fortunate than Winston; and it's entirely possible that had I stayed on in Britain when I first came over at eleven I might have been seduced by the safety of belonging which was only an expression of the absence of a larger idea of human relations.

Human beings can have no existence in isolation from those with whom they share a common destiny, however negatively that destiny is defined. Winston, who was forced into the role of Man Friday by the society of Robinson Crusoes in which he found himself, sought solace where he could. It was a shabby sort of belonging – skin-deep, as it were – and easy enough for me to scorn. I knew that colour alone was not an adequate measure of human beings and that sanctuaries aren't easily achieved, but it was at least a basis for belonging. It was better than no belonging at all, and who was I to judge?

Winston had only ever known Britain. To be more accurate: Winston had only ever known a circumscribed area of Britain, a narrow slip-road with the busy motorway somewhere off in the distance. He was familiar with a few places in the capital city and a limited cross-section of people among whom he worked; but that was all. Even his education at an inner-city comprehensive was worse than useless in this respect, and perhaps it was designed to be so. As far as I could see the school had taught him nothing that could help him when he left, except to work in meaningless jobs. He certainly hadn't been taught that he might want to make something of his life; and yet he was an intelligent, restless man who could have been more than he was.

Winston knew very well that the adopted attitudes at those Blues parties were futile. He knew that none of it mattered to the outside world, to the ordinary British people he worked alongside in those factories, for instance, and whose lives went on regardless, whose lives had always gone on regardless, generation after generation, absorbing the new blood as it came and from wherever it came without even realising what it was doing, unthinking for the most part. An isolated colony cannot exist independently of the dominant culture. Sooner or later the colony is assimilated. The aggressive West Indianness displayed at those Blues parties I went to with Winston, complete with the impenetrable accent and the exaggerated swagger, which even I recognised as a caricature, was, finally, inadequate and purpose-less.

If I had been older at the time I might have said some of this to Winston. But I said nothing; and when I started at college I broke with him. The break wasn't in itself momentous; these things rarely are. One day I just failed to keep an appointment we had made. A week or so later I ran into him in the High Street not far from our old haunt. I had gone to pick up the weekly shopping and I was in a hurry to get home. I was studying for my 'A' levels and I didn't have time to waste wandering the streets or hanging around the bowling alley chatting up women from unlikely places. Even so, I couldn't bring myself to be rude to him and he followed me back to the house; but I was so obviously impatient for him to go that he drank his coffee before it had time to cool and left. He understood very well what had happened, probably more clearly than I was willing to admit. On his way out he gave me a rueful smile and wished me luck. I never saw him again.

I had treated Winston shabbily and I don't suppose we ever forgive ourselves for our cowardly behaviour towards those about whom we care. But I was ambitious; I wanted to get on; I wanted to make something of my life. And I had always known that I would never be content with the life I was expected to live, the life that most people desire: marriage, children, career, the annual holiday; all the externals which help us negotiate our three score and ten. I passed my 'A' levels; I went to university; I went to Canada. I thought I was on my way, and then it turned out to have been a false start. Sometimes, in my cramped room in Notting Hill Gate, in that purple-and-mustard bed-sit with the fold-down formica table and the narrow, lumpy bed, it seemed as if I was back where I was when I first came over six years before. And it was fitting that I should have become friendly with a man who reminded me very strongly of Winston, a man who might in many ways have been Winston ten years on.

Dave lived in nearby Westbourne Grove, just around the corner from me. I called on him three or four times a week. Like Winston, he was from Jamaica; like Winston, he had come over to Britain as a child in the early 1960s. When he left school he worked at a variety of menial jobs, but he had damaged his back lifting a crate in a warehouse and he hadn't worked since. He even qualified for a disability pension although it was difficult to see that there was anything actually wrong with him since his accident didn't appear to stop him from doing any of the things he wanted. This included getting into fights with the Nigerian bouncer at the nearby Blues club just at the time when Nigerians were beginning to muscle in on the London criminal scene and challenge the Yardies, their West Indian counterparts, for a slice of the drugs trade.

The other day I read about one such gang of Nigerian criminals who broke into a man's flat, made him write a suicide note, and then shot him through the heart with a crossbow. I avoided going to these clubs with Dave not because I felt any differently about them – the atmosphere was even more desperate than I remembered from before – but because I was frightened. Dave had the casual approach to violence that has always disturbed me. The world of physical violence is the world of men; men who can't abide violence, who become sick in their stomach when voices are raised and bodies jostled, are ashamed of their fear and try to hide it.

Dave was a tall man, well over six feet, and powerfully built: apart from his receding hairline and a bald patch in the middle of his skull, he even looked like Winston. His girlfriend, Jane, who was white, was twenty years younger. She was short with long black hair that went all the way down her back. When they went out together, which wasn't often, the disparity in their heights was comical: he loped ahead like a knock-kneed panther; she scuttled behind, trying to keep up and never quite managing to do so. She would call out breathlessly from time to time and Dave would slow down, but before long he would revert to his normal stride, his long legs taking two steps to her three.

But they didn't go out much. Sometimes they would go to see a friend, or to score, or to make money in the only way they could. It was only after I had known him a few months that he confided to me how they made that money. Jane would go into a pub and allow a man – well heeled, preferably foreign, usually an Arab – to catch her eye. Then she would lead him into a nearby alley where Dave would be waiting to jump him. It rarely failed.

The money wouldn't be for food or the rent or the electricity bill, all of which were invariably overdue, but for drugs. Any drugs; Dave wasn't particular. The point was to get high. He was high most of the time. It was the easy availability of drugs in the sixties that he always returned to when he spoke of that period. He was proud of the fact that he was one of the first people to have seen Jimi Hendrix live on stage, in a small club off Oxford Street. I don't remember how many times he told me the story of that night and of how he chatted briefly with the great musician between sets. He even tried to imitate the way Hendrix spoke but he wasn't a good mimic. He still had all the original albums, immaculately preserved, the taped recordings of which he played continuously on the stereo system he had recently obtained on a stolen credit card.

Life for him effectively stopped the day that Hendrix died in 1970. I also remembered that day as clearly as he did. It was a fresh, sunny afternoon and I was walking towards Wembley Park Underground when I overheard two people ahead of me discussing Hendrix's death from an overdose of drugs; and it was odd, now, to think of Dave somewhere else in the city at that very moment, a man I didn't know then but who I was destined to know and with whom I already shared a memory of a particular event on a particular day.

Dave also did a little business on the side, but strictly as a go-between. The man in the next room, who worked by day as a court recorder, doubled at night as a dealer. Because this dealer didn't encourage casual customers they would call on Dave instead. He would inflate the price and take a cut and then hustle them out as fast as he could. This was never easy. The junkies especially would insist on shooting up in his room, the blood dripping on the linoleum floor as they jabbed at a vein, which always made Dave livid. Occasionally they would hang around and talk while they waited for the heroin to take effect, deliberately ignoring Dave's anger because that was preferable to the street, at least until the first rush was over.

One such man started crying and told us the story of his friend who recently died. This friend was the British son of Ghanaian parents. For many years he talked about 'going back' to Ghana, of going 'home'. One day he saw a television interview with Jerry Rawlings, the Ghanaian Head of State, which inspired him to do what he had dreamed about for so long. He managed to persuade two English friends from the squat he lived in to go with him; and one can just imagine the three of them doped up to the eyeballs sitting around a dirty kitchen table in a London squat, drinking tea from chipped mugs and getting excited about an unlikely adventure.

But in this case the excitement they generated survived the night. The next day they bought a clapped-out car from a dodgy dealer and headed straight for Dover, just as if they were going up the road to see a friend. The car broke down on the outskirts of London. The Ghanaian's companions, recognising a bad omen for what it was or perhaps just giving expression to the doubts they had anyway, called the whole thing off and hitched back to London. The Ghanaian, keeping his date with destiny, pressed on and somehow or other reached Accra.

For many days he wandered about the capital asking for Rawlings until a policeman took him into custody where he was interrogated, beaten and killed. One doesn't go around asking to see the Head of State in a military regime; one doesn't go around asking to see the Head of State in *any* regime. It so happened that his parents ran into a Ghanaian acquaintance on the London Underground who gave them the tragic news. They immediately began proceedings to fly the body of their dead son back to Britain. Unfortunately, the corpse had already been buried and the authorities weren't sure where the unmarked grave was. Our addict, his speech now slurring as the heroin at last began to take effect, only heard about his friend's death the previous day.

If this man had in effect gone home to die then his journey was wasted; if he had gone to see the land of his father before he died then his journey wasn't wasted. Either way, the story has an odd kind of symmetry. A few months ago, when I was in Accra, I was told that Rawlings, whose father was Scottish, once made the pilgrimage to his ancestral village in the Highlands. When he arrived at the village he came across an ironmongers' with the family name over the door and he asked the man inside where he could find the owner. Blood spoke to blood, as it must and as it always will: even as he was asking he knew that he was talking to his father; his father, recognising his son in turn, recovered rapidly enough from the shock to say that the person he was looking for had sold up and left. I can't vouch for this story, but it would be fitting if it were factually true. In any case, it seems to possess its own, emotional truth.

Dave's place was a sort of refuge for the lost, the broken, the disconnected; men and women who lived shadowy lives on the edge of society and clung to one another with a fierce and sometimes frightening desperation. There was Keith, for instance, Dave's closest friend. He was from one of the smaller Caribbean islands and lived nearby with his girlfriend, a small, mousy woman who was once married to a stockbroker. I never did find out what happened, whether she left the semi in Surrey of her own accord or whether she was forced out by her upwardly mobile husband.

Whatever the case she made me realise that one didn't have to be black and/or born in the West Indies (or Australia, for that matter) to be an outsider in Britain. Obvious outsiders have a tendency to reserve exclusively for themselves the status of difference, a handicap which is used in moments of self-pity to berate those denying you your rightful place in the sun. In fact she was just as much of an outsider as Keith or the Australian in Earls Court; but in overlooking her predicament I began to realise the extent to which I was still assuming colour, if not birth, to operate at a level I thought I had already rejected. And perhaps her case was the more dramatic *because* she was white and British but an outsider nonetheless.

She had been with Keith for seven years. In all that time she hadn't seen her children. Sometimes Keith would disappear for weeks or even months at a time but he always came back. Even when he went to prison she visited him as often as she could and turned down the succession of men, Keith's friends all of them, who called on her thinking she would be an easy lay. She had a sad smile. I never saw her throw her head back and laugh. Mostly she just sat quietly sipping the tea she never refused while Keith regaled anyone who would listen with his latest exploits.

Here they all came to Dave's place: there was the ex-boxer who was just out of prison and had been wandering about in a drunken haze for twenty-four hours. He turned up at five in the morning, a big, powerful man just beginning to go to seed with approaching middle-age. He didn't smile at all and never raised his voice above a whisper as he chain-smoked, the cigarette pinched between thumb and forefinger, the smoke curling upwards either side of his big, fleshy hand with the broken knuckles and the manicured fingernails. He had a way of looking at you that made you realise he was capable of sticking a knife in your guts as easily as he would strike a match.

He was one of those people who live in a continuous present. For such people, the past and the future don't exist as discrete parcels of time which have a direct bearing on what you do, and so they never make the connection between an action and its likely consequences. Such people are mad, but it's a madness made more chilling by their seeming ability to function at a day-to-day level. He didn't hear voices or see apparitions; he didn't have a need to rape little girls. He was perfectly capable of finding himself a room and organising some money as and when he needed. But he was mad all the same. He was mad with hate. Life had sucked the pity out of him and now he didn't care.

Here they all came to Dave's place: there was Jane's friend – also white, also British, also an outsider – who had just had an abortion, her fourth or fifth or sixth. She was only nineteen and she spoke incessantly about her mother, though not always directly; like most people she talked in code so that you had to read between the lines of what she said. But perhaps this is how we all talk; perhaps it is the only way we can communicate what we most deeply feel.

It seems that Jane's friend was kicked out by her mother the first time she became pregnant, and now she threw herself at one man after another as she was discarded by each in turn. Every time I saw her she was with someone different, and each time you could see that she had let herself in for more trouble. It couldn't be otherwise. The pattern was set. She would always attract unsuitable men, and they would always abuse her. She wasn't the brightest of people but she had a sweet, placid nature. I liked her and I felt sorry for her, but there was nothing I could do to help her.

After these people left, usually well after midnight, Jane would rub out the specks of blood before we settled down to a game of poker. The stakes were small – pennies really – but it helped to pass the time, of which we had plenty. I stopped playing cards with them the night I caught Dave stealing a five-pence piece from my pile when I briefly looked away. At the time I pretended I hadn't seen, although Jane, who glanced quickly in my direction at the critical moment, suspected that I had. She hoped I wouldn't say anything and I didn't, but for a long time afterwards I thought about Dave's behaviour and wondered what had impelled him to do it. I was under no illusions about his 'honour', a prohibitively expensive commodity in so wretched a life, but five pounds would have made better sense.

As I thought about Dave's trivial theft and my own initial lack of surprise I came to understand his behaviour as a measure of his alienation and not personal to me; his relationship with me – with anybody, even Jane – was dictated by the absence of any sense of rootedness. Without that rootedness he lacked the framework for a system of values by which he could live. Human beings disintegrate without structures. They become treacherous and they thieve, even from their friends.

But in Britain, a country with powerful institutions, such individual excesses are only ever practised by a minority, whose own psychic disintegration has reached the point where they are no longer able to function with sufficient restraint. Later, in Nigeria, I was to see how an entire nation of thieves could be created by the absence of structures in the public sphere, and this despite the existence of undeniably powerful institutions in the private sphere.

'Few men realise that their life, the very essence of their character, their capabilities and their audacities, are only the expression of their belief in the safety of their surroundings.' It took Joseph Conrad, a Pole who settled in Britain and wrote in English, to understand this. Dave could steal from me because, in the end, there was nothing to stop him from doing so; there was no *internal* reason why he shouldn't steal.

One sees the evidence of this alienation among a relatively high proportion of younger British-Caribbeans in the streets of all our cities. The other day I was waiting for a friend at a tube station. It was lunchtime. The ticket-collector had gone for his break and there was no one to replace him. Most of the commuters simply dropped their used tickets into the box provided. I was there for half an hour. In that time three young men seized their opportunity to gather a handful of these used tickets and stuff them in their pockets.

Why? What did they hope to achieve? One free ride, perhaps? But that wasn't important, any more than the small amount was important, any more than my five-pence piece was important to Dave. The most positive thing that can be said is that it was criminal activity and as such an act of defiance, which is all that is left to the outsider. Such people have great difficulty finding their way into the mainstream of society. This is made harder in a society which is already coping with great change. More is demanded from the individual in terms of talent and energy, qualities which can more easily be developed from a secure base.

So it was with Dave. He didn't lock into society at any point. And if I was attracted to him because he reflected something of my own condition, he was also dangerous to me for that reason. I wasn't as deeply alienated as he was but I understood his predicament and I could identify with it. For his part, Dave assumed that my understanding reflected a deeper connection than I knew to be the case. This was partly an expression of his own need, partly a result of my own successful projection. We became close. He even encouraged me to sleep with Jane, entrusting her to me one night so that he could chase after another woman who had recently been giving him the come-on. For a brief, intense period we were almost brothers.

And then I left. I couldn't stand the life I was leading, a purposeless existence that wasn't producing anything or getting me anywhere. My world had shrunk to two rooms – mine and Dave's – and the short distance between them; and in the atmosphere of drugs and petty crime and the company of losers it would have been easy, because I lacked sufficient internal ballast, to be sucked in by it and to imagine that this was all there was, that a more meaningful life, the life of the people who hurried past me in the street on their way to their jobs or their families or their week-ends in the country, was a life to which only other people had an entrée.

Dave and Jane and Keith and Keith's girlfriend and I were all excluded. We could have no place in such a world. We lived in a lesser, parallel world, but we thought it was whole because we couldn't see its poverty. We affected contempt for those who didn't inhabit bleak rooms or watch the afternoon soaps on television, but even as we too-frequently told ourselves these things I knew that it was all a colossal lie repeated only for the sake of our own reassurance.

I went back to Swansea. It was a smaller and more manageable place and there was a woman. She was British and she was to teach me many things about her country (and mine), but slowly, obliquely and painfully: in order to see the world as she saw it and to hear the things she was telling me I had to open myself up; I had to let down my guard and examine my hysteria; I had to become myself.

By and by we went to live in Ireland, in an isolated farmhouse four miles from the village of Ballydehob in the extreme south-west. It wasn't a calculated move, more a chance meeting with a man who had bought a small-holding but couldn't move in immediately and wanted the house occupied for a nominal rent. He didn't tell us that there was no electricity, or that the running water consisted of one cold tap in the lean-to-kitchen through which the wind howled on dark winter evenings and the cold stone floor froze the soles of your feet. On the day we arrived, our belongings crammed into a 35-cwt, the neighbouring farmer was heating the pig swill on the range while chickens wandered in and out of the open door. It wasn't an auspicious beginning but we couldn't turn back. We decided to give it six months and we stayed three years.

We soon became part of the established settler community of Europeans and North Americans, mostly young, who had rejected what they saw as the intolerably materialist culture of modern life for the more human values of the rural scene. I didn't share their vision of Babylon, not least because human life everywhere is, *ipso facto*, materialistic; and I knew very well that those societies which were less successful in this regard were doing their best to achieve the same level of physical comfort, beginning with food and shelter and ending with the sophisticated technology. In the meantime, we grew our own food, dug our own turf, and told ourselves how much healthier was the life we were leading.

It was in Ireland, ironically, that I kept a garden for the first time and began to understand something of the English – as opposed to British – passion for gardening. The Celts don't appear to have elevated the idea of the garden to the level of a national aesthetic. The garden in England transcends even class and reveres the famous practitioners (or, properly, artists) of the past.

If my father had been English I would doubtless have inherited this passion as a perfectly ordinary part of my childhood, but my father thought it beneath him to do any manual labour and he employed a gardener instead. My mother, who was Scottish, did keep a few potted plants on the verandah because, after all, she was brought up in England; but after she left they died from lack of care and one day the gardener, whose only job it was to cut the grass with a hand-blade, the sweat pouring off his body and soaking his torn khaki shorts as he swished a series of arcs in the hot afternoon sun, was told to throw them away.

Now I understood how soothing it was to go into the garden and potter about and watch the seeds you had sown a few weeks before slowly inch their way up through the soil. The most I had done before was occasionally mow the lawn in the back garden of our house in Wembley, and then it was always a chore carried out under protest. Now I proudly displayed the neat rows of lettuce and sweet pea and turnip as I discussed with friends the advantages of this or that way of making compost.

The garden itself, about a quarter of an acre, was once

an orchard. The gooseberry bushes still survived, eight of them in two rows of four, as had the blackberries which surrounded the plot. I dug over the garden in the evenings after a day's work on the building site in the village four miles away, the sun slowly setting behind the hills in the distance: I had never looked at a sunset before. I even acquired my own robin, just as it said I would in the book on organic gardening. Naturally we were all organic gardeners. For this reason we couldn't eat carrots because of the carrot fly, from which there was no organic protection. 'I haven't eaten a carrot in seven years,' a friend said solemnly one day, and we nodded in sympathy.

I even grew vegetables I thought I didn't like just for the sake of growing them. Cauliflower was one such. I had eaten cauliflower cheese in Nigeria but it was prepared by Alexander, our cook, at my mother's insistence and he didn't have any idea what it should look or even taste like. To Alexander it was hardly proper (Nigerian, that is) food. My mother, who hated waste or perhaps wanted to maintain the fiction that she *could* have an everyday British meal in the tropics, pretended that everything was fine. Everything wasn't fine. It tasted awful. I swore then that I would never eat cauliflower again; but early one winter morning in Ireland I went into the garden I had dug and saw the most beautiful cauliflower head, beautiful against the cold white earth and the bare brown trees. All it needed was to be cooked by a European who knew what to do with it.

Life in Ireland was attractive, not least because I was happy to leave behind the whole business of colour. The Irish apparently didn't see colour. They only saw me as another settler. This was a tremendous liberation. In Britain one is forced to be constantly aware of colour, even when you tell yourself that you don't care and that you're damned if you're going to live your life by other people's precepts. But the collective consciousness isn't so easily dismissed, unless you live the life of a hermit. As long as you live in society the collective won't let you alone.

For a long time after I came to Britain I told myself that I didn't care about colour and what other people thought. This wasn't true. I did care. I cared very much, but it wasn't until I started this essay that I realised the extent to which it troubled me. At first I was determined to ignore the race issue – as it's euphemistically called – and write about Britain colour-blind, but when I read over the first draft I was disturbed at the extent to which it had entered the narrative, even against my will.

I cared more than I had imagined. I cared so much, in fact, that I soon realised that any book I wrote about Britain would have to begin and end with colour. I resented this because I could see clearly enough the ways in which I was thereby trapped into doing what all 'black' writers were supposed to do, which was to write about race. It was my place, hence the term 'black writer'. Nobody called Martin Amis a white writer. He was normal; he was just a writer; he could write about anything he pleased.

I was also uneasy about the complications of language. Take the word 'black'. Human beings so described range from very black to almost white. Strictly speaking, few of them are black; they are only perceived as such in Britain because colour is seen from the perspective of not-white, white being the norm. But in Nigeria 'white' is perceived as not-black, black in this case being the corresponding norm. So in Britain I am black – unless I'm mistaken for an Arab; and in Nigeria, where they know a black man when they see one, I am white – unless I'm mistaken for a Lebanese. What am I, then? Perhaps, not-black-not-white. And yet it was colour which emphasised my apart-ness in my own country. This disturbed me in Nigeria almost as much as it did in Britain, the only – and crucial – difference being that in Nigeria it was never a threat, merely a curiosity when it wasn't a positive advantage.

To be white in Africa is to possess power. You come from a settled, prosperous world which produces motor cars and aeroplanes and the currencies which can buy these things. By contrast, Africa produces political instability, famine and civil war. As a child in what was still a colonial dependency I took an obscure pride in identifying with my mother's country. At a less anguished level, this was because the mass of Nigerians thought of me as white. *Oyinbo* (white man), the children used to chant at my brothers and me whenever we went out with our parents. If I was a foreigner in my father's country because I was a different colour it followed that I really was to be identified with Britain, the colonial power.

Much later, after I left Nigeria and after my father died, I began to understand that I had inherited something of my father's own complex responses towards this whole business, the doubts he had of his worth as a man. He had spent ten years in Britain studying medicine at a time when there were no laws on racial abuse. 'What? Speak up, you're not in the jungle now; can't you talk proper English?'; and this on the upper deck of a London bus. He himself never mentioned any of this. It was my mother who recounted some of the scenes they met with whenever they went out together; and I wondered at the humiliation it must have been for him to be with a woman and to have to pretend to be unconcerned, which was the only way he could salvage his dignity. He was hardly the kind of man who could get into a street fight, and by temperament he tended to bottle things up and then meditate at length on the insult to that dignity. He was a proud man.

I also began to understand my father's marriage to my mother in terms of the power she conferred on him by proxy. A white wife was a symbol of his arrival. He was an ambitious man who had embraced the European world in order to realise that ambition. My mother was part of the package. He could go back to Lagos with a European profession and a European wife and be as good as any of the Europeans who ran the country, beginning with the European doctor less qualified than he but who remained in charge of the hospital in which he worked until the day independence was declared and my father took over. It was a long, humiliating haul but he made it. The price of that achievement came later, but the price of failure would have been higher again: the brother with whom he travelled abroad, also to study medicine, fooled about with his future and now drives a cab in New York.

What, then, was I to make of the fact that in my mother's country I was seen as black? My immediate response was to tell myself that I didn't care, that the subject of colour bored me and that colour wasn't important anyway. I repeated this to myself for years, beginning with my adventures with Winston at those Blues parties; and then I started to write about Britain, about my mother's country and what it meant to me, and I realised that the issue was absolutely central.

But in the process I had at least avoided the ultimate trap of allowing the fact of colour to consume all else, which is what happens when it's the only thing you do think about, when you allow colour to mark the boundaries of your horizon and overshadow all else. My instincts were right to the extent that colour could not be the sole definition of my relationship with my mother's country, and that to permit it more space than it deserved would be to distort my inheritance. One's inheritance simply can't be reduced to the colour of one's skin.

'I went to Jamaica for the first time earlier this year and I didn't like it. It was hot and dirty and poor and they couldn't understand what I was saying most of the time.' The assertive note in the south London accent wouldn't have been necessary but that the 22-year-old speaker, a trainee telephone engineer, just happened to have a Jamaican father. In fact he was only a working-class Londoner visiting the Third World on a tourist package.

I liked his candour. When he saw that I didn't react in the way he was presumably used to, when he under-stood that I didn't expect him to feel guilty because he didn't think all blacks – any more than all whites – were brothers or sisters, he softened and recounted his first meeting with his grandmother in a room in a village some miles out of Kingston. She was very old and near death. She opened her eyes when he came in and pointed to the photos of him on the bedside table: as a baby; his first day at school; on holiday at the seaside; Christmas last year.

This image of his grandmother was especially moving within the context of his fidelity regarding Jamaica and what it meant to him. He didn't corrupt the experience with sentimentality, which is what happens when we betray the truth because we cannot bear the pain of conflicting emotions, a form of squeamishness like not taking the life of an animal in great pain in order to avoid killing. And at the root of such squeamishness is a profound self-pity which enables us to hide the pain from ourselves and adopt attitudes we don't feel and mouth slogans we don't believe because the pain won't leave us alone and, after all, somebody must be responsible.

In *The European Tribe*, a recent book by a 'black' British writer, Caryl Phillips tells us that he came to Britain 'at the portable age of twelve weeks'. His book is based on the premise that Europe is a single, coherent entity, and that what can be said of one country can be said of all: 'I could not believe that the British were really any different from the French, or the Spanish from the Swedish.' This is a little problematical – the British are *not* like the French, or the Spanish like either, never mind the Swedes – but his concern is with the fact of colour, and what this means to him as a European. This is the dominant theme of his travelogue, and it is stated clearly enough at the beginning: 'The fundamental problem was, if I was going to continue to live in Britain, how was I to reconcile the contradiction of feeling British, while being told in many subtle and unsubtle ways that I did not belong?'

In the course of his travels he finds himself standing on a bridge in Venice and meditating on Othello. In the process he discovers – but the juxtaposition is awkward; the book itself awkwardly constructed – that the sight of so much beauty leaves him unmoved: 'I was raised in Europe but Venice looked strangely distant and eerie.' Back in Britain at the end of his journey, having travelled through Spain, France, Holland, Germany, Norway, Poland and the Soviet Union, he returns again to that melancholy moment in Italy: 'I was raised in Europe, but as I walked the streets of Venice, with all their self-evident beauty, I felt nothing. Unlike Othello,

I am culturally of the West. I stood on the Rialto and thought how much more difficult it must have been for him, possessing a language and a past that were still present. Nothing inside me stirred to make me rejoice, "Ours is a rich culture", or "I'm a part of this".'

The tragedy implicit in this statement, which is indeed worthy of Shakespeare, is terrifying. The author is describing the condition of a person who exists in nothingness – no connections; no supports; life lived in limbo. This is difficult to conceive and might even be a description of madness. Is it really possible for a person to grow up in a country and feel nothing whatsoever towards it: to ignore the sharp, acrid smell of smoke on a winter's evening as you walk to the pub on the corner; to be unmoved by a beautiful sunset when you drive in the country on a summer's day; to be cold to the sound of English in your ears when you return from abroad? And all this in the only country you have ever known? The language which has taught you to look and to hear and to speak? I don't believe it's possible; I don't believe it's among the human possibilities: the violence is too deep.

Two telling incidents are described in the book. The first – 'one of the most painful episodes of my childhood' – occurs in the opening chapter. One day at school the English teacher decides to explain the origins of some of the pupils' surnames: 'So Greenberg was Jewish, Morley originally came from the small Yorkshire town of the same name, McKenzie was a Scot.' Eventually it is Phillips's turn. The teacher informs him that he must be Welsh. 'The whole class laughed, while I stared back at him stony-faced, knowing full well that I was not from Wales. The truth was I had no idea where I was from . . .' In the classroom, then, among people 'I considered my friends', his identity is an occasion for humour.

The second incident occurs in adulthood, at a function in a London publishing house. An editor, who perhaps does not realise that the author is within hearing distance, refers to him as a 'jungle bunny'. Phillips does not record how the others around this person responded, so we must assume that they said nothing, as is the British way. Even among the liberal intelligentsia, then, in the company of people who read books or are supposed to read books, the author is made to feel different, alien, a person out of whom money can be made but who, despite his British passport and his Oxford degree and his English accent, doesn't belong, isn't one of us – a jungle bunny. Of course he is hurt. But is that enough? Has he thereby addressed the central question, which is the undeniable fact of his Britishness, and this despite or even because of other people's perceptions?

He's British, after all: that is the point. I remember when I lived in Wembley I became friendly with the man next door, an Englishman (white) in his early forties. His name was Alan. He had thin, sharp features, thinning hair and a jaunty walk: he said he had once been a merchant seaman, but had left when he got married. He worked on the same trading estate as I did so that we often walked home together. He was fond of walking: during that summer we went for a stroll most evenings, but it was a long time before I appreciated summer as a time of warmth and light. I was still used to the absolute regularity of the tropics where the sun rises every morning at six and night comes suddenly twelve hours later. I had to go through many winters in Britain to see summer as a magical time, and to understand the meaning of the old mid-summer festivals.

One day Alan asked me about my plans. In that gushing way of adolescence I told him I was going to university. He laughed. A week later, after I had ignored him repeatedly, refusing to walk with him and not answering when he spoke to me, he sidled up to me as I was leaving the house and said something about blacks. So it was out at last, but what was it to me? Who was Alan that my well-being should be determined by his good opinion? If this was the worst he could do then it was easy enough to deal with. What was more, I could even deal with the idea of lots of Alans, all of them seeing me as he did, and to hold this alongside the other idea that his country was mine also whatever he and his kind said or thought or felt about me.

It was a relief, in Ireland, to be free of the racial business. This had as much to do with the sentiments of the settler community in which I found myself as it did with the genuine innocence of the Irish: people were people and not to be seen in terms of colour. However, the Irish had their own bigotry; and if living in Ireland was personally liberating for me, the same couldn't be said for the young Irish couple, one Protestant, the other Catholic, who committed joint suicide because of the pressures which had turned the six counties of the north into a state of civil war.

That was the second suicide which occurred while we were there. The first was that of an Englishman who had already been living in Ireland for ten years by the time we arrived. Sam left Britain after his Ph. D. as part of the hippy dream to go back to the land, but he was the least practical man I have ever met. He certainly wasn't cut out to be a small-holder. He had an idea that he wanted to be a writer and he even wrote a few poems and stories and first chapters of novels, but they didn't amount to much. He had a certain facility with words which impressed those who didn't know any better, but that was all: he expressed pedestrian ideas in pedestrian language; he hadn't begun to think about what he wanted to say and so he hadn't needed to find the language in which to say it. His work was clichéd. He relied on his facility alone and talked to people who knew less than he did.

As the years passed and it seemed he wasn't getting anywhere he started to panic. He thought that perhaps he had made the wrong decision. He turned forty and had nothing to show for it, and he knew that it was too late to start a 'proper' career. And then, quite un-expectedly, his father had a heart attack and Sam was required to go to London. His parents were central European Jews who had fled Germany in the 1930s and quickly established a business importing electrical goods. With his father's heart attack they could no longer manage on their own but they were reluctant to sell up after the years of hard work which had paid off. Their only other son, Sam's younger brother, lived in an ashram in Surbiton and went about in orange robes.

I'm not sure what happened to Sam in London. Perhaps he was suddenly re-acquainted with the tension between his own Britishness and his parents' foreign origins, made starker by his public school education; perhaps he realised the inadequacy with which he had come to terms with the split engendered in him since childhood; perhaps his parents had a way of reminding him – by a look, a gesture, a pointed question: 'And what is it that you're doing, exactly?' – of the money they had wasted and the failure he had become. Sam returned after two months with a monstrous depression. He had suddenly aged. His hair was greyer and his shoulders sagged, and it was a perpetual effort to keep his attention. I heard later that he tried to hang himself in his parents' attic but his mother discovered him. He was bundled back to Ireland. Depression turned to paranoia. When he received a letter from the insurance company reminding him that the annual premium was overdue he thought that people were trying to burn the house down and he told everybody to hide under the table.

He became obsessed with money. He found a job as a driver and put in so much overtime that sometimes he wouldn't get back until two or three in the morning and be up again at six. And all the while he was applying for jobs. With every rejection he became more and more withdrawn. He didn't talk to anybody, not even to his wife. One day he borrowed a shot-gun from the local farmer. He said he wanted to shoot rabbits. Early the next morning, about five o'clock, his wife was woken by a blast nearby. She went outside and found him slumped against the shed in the back. He had put the shot-gun in his mouth and blown his brains out.

Growing vegetables on a small-holding wasn't for Sam. He was an intellectual; he should have stayed in the university where he had studied for his doctorate. Sam's world was the world of books. Living the simple life was just an idea which excited him at a time when people were talking about such things. But it was only an idea. In the end Ireland trapped him. He had no other connection with the place except this idea; and he gradually discovered – and how delicately he would have been attuned to it – that just because the people spoke English didn't mean that Ireland was like Britain. Ireland was a different country. Quite how much so was sometimes disguised *because* they spoke English. Sam was a stranger, an outsider. He didn't belong except among a small group of people who were themselves outsiders, people who were defined by the fact that they were not-Irish.

For their part, the Irish were remarkably tolerant of these settlers, some of whom could be grossly insensitive to local mores. There were those who made a big deal about swimming in the nude or breastfeeding in the bars and would then pretend that these were ethical issues when it was pointed out to them that the locals found such behaviour offensive. In any case, people who believed in nude bathing as an expression of their personality shouldn't have moved to a country where it rained most of the time. I remember it rained solidly for the first two weeks we were there, a fine drizzle that never let up and which prompted the greeting, 'It's a fine, soft day' from the farmers you passed in the lane. Soft was indeed the word: the land squelched beneath your wellington boots and your clothes were permanently damp.

The rain aside, there were times when Ireland reminded me more of Nigeria than Britain. There was the same extended family arrangement where everybody was your cousin, no matter how distant, and there was the same place of the religious as an integral part of everyday life. This sense of a tightly-knit community bound by shared moral values which transcended political ideologies was missing in Britain, which was what the settlers identified as their reason for coming. They didn't say it quite like this. They spoke instead about the materialism and decadence of modern British life (sentiments I was to hear echoed almost word for word by Nigerians when I made a trip there a few years later), but the irony was that most of the settlers were themselves stamped very firmly in the secular mode.

I never heard of any who attended either of the local churches, for example, or took part in the religious festivals, Protestant or Catholic, of which there were many. One group even tried to start their own school because they disliked the emphasis on religious education in the state curriculum. This insult to the local community, calculated or otherwise (though mostly otherwise), reminded me of nothing so much as the attitude of the British expatriates in colonial Nigeria who didn't want their children mixing with the children of the natives. When Nigerians like my father started sending their children to the same schools the expatriates finally realised that the Empire was over and left.

But the culture-clash in Ireland was partly the difference between the city and the country. Most of the settlers came from the big metropolitan centres, from London and Berlin and New York, the places where the degeneracy of modern life was apparently reaching its apotheosis and which for that reason were at the point of collapse. 'Do you know how many times I was mugged in my own flat?' one American was fond of saying whenever two or more were gathered together; but in many ways the move was too extreme. In common with a number of the settlers, she would have been more at home in Dublin than Ballydehob; and perhaps if they had themselves come from rural communities they mightn't have felt the gap they identified in their lives.

We had the misfortune to live next door to a family which, in their backwardness and bloody-mindedness, summed up the worst in rural life. Late one evening the elder daughter came round to say that 'Daddy' wanted to talk to . . . She spoke quickly and I didn't catch what she said, but since a strict sexual apartheid operated as a general rule I assumed it was me he wanted and I prepared to go. Then she repeated, more firmly this time, 'No, Daddy wants to speak to *herself*'.

It transpired that our neighbour had promised to take his wife to her mother's that evening but suddenly decided, while they were milking the cows, that he didn't feel like taking her after all. She shouted at him, he hit her with the milk pail, and now, three hours later, she was still sobbing in the kitchen. Obviously this was one of the eternal mysteries of women which could only be solved by another woman. It never occurred to him that he could talk to his wife, or even that he might have been at fault in the first place. Meanwhile, the inevitable brother (all Irish famhouses had an unmarried brother), who had never been further than the nearby town in his fifty years and only then for a minor operation, was calmly sitting at the kitchen table waiting for his tea.

Our neighbours were particularly cranky. This was partly because, as Protestants, they were themselves outsiders of sorts. One of the reasons the brother remained a bachelor was because there were so few Protestant families in the area. A man had to go great distances to find a wife, which meant that he also had to go great distances when his wife inexplicably wanted to visit her mother. Because the Protestants were a small community they tended to be insular and suspicious. The Catholics, who possessed the unequivocal confidence of belonging, were far more open; and if they took offence at some of the excesses of the settlers, they were too delicate to let it show. This wasn't hypocrisy because they weren't a hypocritical people. When the Dublin drug squad decided enough was enough and descended, many locals stood by those who were busted for growing marijuana in their greenhouses.

Ireland was a neutral country for me; and it was in Ireland, away from the pressures of the race issue in Britain, that I was able to extend what I had begun in that purple-and-mustard room in Notting Hill Gate. By then I had given up writing novels, the manuscripts of which I burned in the yard one autumn evening as the moon rose in a clear sky, the dedication to the fire god being a sort of purification rite and the symbol of a new beginning. Where I had previously written long novels I now wrote extremely short stories. All the stories, which might better be called vignettes, centred on incidents I recalled from my childhood in Nigeria. I think I understood then, but vaguely, that I had to clear the backlog of one inheritance before I could properly explore the implications of the other. To do so I had to remove myself from either, but after three years it was time to return. Growing vegetables simply wasn't enough. To have stayed longer would have been a form of escape.

There was also the children to consider. The children of the settler community were in a difficult position. They were as marginalised in the society as were their parents, but they were forced to cope more directly with the consequences of their marginalisation. They lived one life at home and another at school, and as they grew older the question of their identity, of who they were and where they belonged, became more urgent. This revealed itself most directly in the problem of what they would do with themselves when they left school. Some of the older children started to run wild, as if it was they who were carrying the burden of their parents' choices. Many of the parents didn't see what was happening by pretending that everything was OK.

When we returned to Britain, this time to Birmingham, I saw Dave again but only on the few occasions I was able to travel to London. Things were different, of course: the nature of the bond between us could hardly have withstood such a long break. In the time I was away he and Jane had been allocated a council flat in Ladbroke Grove. It was typical of Dave, who had hardly been out of London in twenty years, that even in the capital he lived within a manageable radius. This was the measure of his insecurity about his surroundings, a life given meaning only by way of a reductive geography: these streets, those houses, this pub; familiar landmarks that could be traversed in the space of a single afternoon, like the circumference of his own stoned consciousness.

How little immigrants know of the country in which they find themselves. Dave told me that he had once been to Cardiff on a day-trip but hadn't liked it; and I had to admit that the image of him sitting on a coach in the middle of the M4 was oddly disconcerting, as if he had suddenly been catapulted into enemy territory and was in some kind of personal danger. This is perhaps an odd way of perceiving what ought to have been a simple day's outing, and unremarkable enough in itself. The day-trip – the family excursion to the seaside or to an historic town – is a peculiarly British activity. But Dave belonged to the anonymity of the city, which can more easily accommodate the outsider. And not just any part of the city: Westbourne Grove, Notting Hill Gate, Ladbroke Grove; these were among the areas that had been designated for the displaced.

Now Dave had a child. I have a mental picture of him sitting on the floor of the living room with his daughter on his lap, riveted to some nonsense on the big colour television set. One advantage of living in Britain, and the reason why he had come over in the first place, was that it provided him with the material security he lacked back home. This society housed, clothed, and fed him, and would educate his child and look after her if and when she fell ill. Nothing was required of him but to sit at home and keep out of trouble. This was the hallmark of a wealthy and secure society, and it makes nonsense of all the left-wing talk of revolution, in itself a form of play and tolerated as such by the powers that be.

The people who were supposed to take part in the overthrow of the elected government; the people who were supposedly impelled to act out of some fantastically elaborate idea of historical necessity, were busy watching television at eleven o'clock in the morning: 'Never has any country given its people so many toys to play with or sent such highly gifted individuals to the remotest corners of idleness, as close as possible to the frontiers of pain,' Saul Bellow says of American society, but he may as well have been talking about modern Britain. Dave even had his daily comic. It was open on the racing page on the floor beside him, with pencil ticks beside the horses he fancied. I have yet to meet another man who gave me such a powerful sense of life lived with the sole purpose of killing time. Every action he undertook was in the nature of a flight from eternity – that rough beast threatening to devour him even as he rocked his daughter to a fragile sleep.

One day I heard that he had been busted. The police, acting on a tip, broke down his door and found a carrier bag stuffed with cocaine. He claimed that the bag had been left there without his knowledge. By some miracle – even Dave had his portion of luck – he wasn't sent down, and this despite his refusal to reveal that it had been left there by his friend, Keith. So there was honour of sorts after all, even more than one would find among people who did not steal five-pence pieces. Or perhaps I'm being sentimental; perhaps Keith had paid him to keep quiet. Dave wouldn't have charged much for the service rendered.

Some time after his trial my brother ran into him in the pub in Notting Hill Gate where we used to drink, an anonymous place on the Bayswater Road with dim lights and plush velvet decor and tables which doubled as computer games. He told my brother that he and Jane had separated and that he was sleeping on a friend's floor in Westbourne Grove, two houses down from his previous place, until he could fix up something more permanent. This seemed to stand as a comment on his inability to move, as if he was condemned to go round and round in circles without ever breaking out. He couldn't move forward; he hadn't moved in twenty years.

The journey from the West Indies, undertaken with what hope I don't know because he never said and I never asked, had broken Dave's life in two. There is a Czech song which says that exile means being born again, but without the comforts of childhood. Dave had been formed in one society and he was living in another. Everything that he had learnt as a child – the names of the trees; the smell of the earth after rain; the quality of the light at sunset: everything that had gone to make him the man he was – could no longer be of any use to him here. He was fractured. That was why he couldn't act in any meaningful way. He may as well have been physically paralysed, and in a sense he was: he suffered from paralysis of the will.

It would have been easier if Dave was blessed with a special talent. He could have used that talent, the discipline it would have entailed and the rigorous choices it would have forced on him, to try and understand the nature of his fate. But he was just an ordinary man whose fate demanded exceptional responses. That was the nature of his tragedy; and it was no small part of it that he had come to an old country in which recent arrivals could have no place. I knew something about old countries. Nigeria was an old country. And it wasn't until I lived in Canada, a new country, that I grasped what this meant.

It had been easy in Canada. I don't only mean by this that Canadians spoke English and had recognisably European institutions. That was also true of Nigeria. What I mean is that the society was unformed, fluid; the earth itself didn't speak of blood and generations; the earth didn't speak of history – at least not in a language they could understand. The only truly indigenous Canadians were the Eskimos and the North American Indians, but their cultures had been fatally broken – like the Australian Aborigines, perhaps, or the long-extinct Arawaks of the Caribbean – and now they wandered the cities like a lost tribe in search of their own destruction. The men were drunk by mid-day and the women could be had for the price of a beer. They constituted the most depressing sight in what was otherwise a stunningly beautiful country.

Canadians had no strong sense of themselves as a distinct people; the discrete groups which made up the country retained allegiance to older and more established societies from which they had only recently come. There were Canadians from Czechoslovakia and from Ireland and from Jamaica; their identity as Canadians was given reality only in terms of that other society. The second and third generations, although born and raised in Canada, inherited this double allegiance along with their surnames and their mothers' cooking.

Canadians continually betrayed their need for re-assurance in the way they were forever asking strangers what they thought of their country at the same time as they made sure to mention their own special ancestry, as if they could only be validated through the eyes of another who in turn had to be provided with clues suggesting a more complex history. The British, who do not doubt their identity, rarely ask foreigners their opinion of Britain. When they do so it is invariably out of politeness. They aren't much interested in the answer, and care little what the visitor thinks. They are secure enough in themselves, when the foreigner misunderstands the question and launches into a tirade – obsession with the past; rigid class structure; neurotic levels of official secrecy – to shrug their shoulders in pity or contempt. At best they will make sympathetic noises while they look around for a means of escape; at worst (but rarely: the British are nothing if not polite) they will tell them to go back where they came from.

As with all old countries, Britain is exclusive. It doesn't easily make room for outsiders. Outsiders, in turn, quickly discover that there is no place for them; and the only way they can cope with what looks very much like rejection is to conclude that the British are a cold and unfriendly people, just like their weather. The fact that the British are reserved, and that this reserve is often mistaken for hostility, only compounds the misunderstanding. Nigerians, who are not reserved, are no less exclusive, a fact which escapes foreigners who suddenly discover, even after many years in the country, that the apparent volubility they found perfectly charming – 'so different from stuffy old England', as one expatriate said to me – is only a mask easily shed. That same expatriate, after ten years in the country, was later forced to return to Britain for personal reasons and quickly discovered how little he was missed in his adopted country.

Dave was forever telling me how much he hated the British, but I didn't believe him because I knew how little he knew about them and so misread the signals. In any case, understanding wouldn't have helped him since he didn't have a means of entry. Britain is full of outsiders who nevertheless become an integral part of the society by virtue of their talent. This is the other side of a country which, sufficiently confident in itself, can easily make space for those who have something to offer. John Fashanu can play football for England and V. S. Naipaul is regarded as a British writer. There is nothing strange in either fact although Paul Theroux, in his own book on Britain, *The Kingdom by the Sea*, regards this as a typical example of British hypocrisy:

> Policemen were 'coloured', convicted criminals were 'West Indian', and purse-snatchers were 'nig-nogs'. But when a black runner came first in a race against foreigners he was 'English'. If he came second he was 'British'. If he cheated he was 'West Indian'.

I've never believed that the British are any more – or any less – hypocritical than other nations. Besides, one could just as well examine Theroux's assertion from the other side: the fact that the black runner can be regarded as English – or British – whatever the confusions over nomenclature.

Not that Dave could offer anything exceptional. He was just himself, an ordinary man in an extraordinary situation who had the good fortune to find himself in a society of plenty, where a base level of security is taken for granted and the shops are bursting with food. And for Dave, a man from a poor society who knew plenty when he saw it, not even the complicated and unwelcome burden (or imposition) of colour could drive him away. He was an absolute outsider. Colour was only a distraction which operated to emphasise but not define his position in the society. He may as well have come from Australia and he would have been just as much an outsider as the man I met in the pub in Earls Court. For Dave, Britain was home only because he happened to live here; it was not home in any wider sense. And it was inevitable, in the end, that we should go our separate ways. Dave's place was never really my scene.

2

The dream of a common language

I did feel he was different from me because of his colour; the feeling I had came from way back, something to do with childhood or reading *Uncle Tom's Cabin*. I wasn't ashamed of it; just cowardly about mentioning it on television when the words might come out wrong.

Beryl Bainbridge: *English Journey*.

'Would you like to come to England?' My mother was standing in the doorway of the bathroom. It was mid-day, December: the rains were still three months away. When the rains did come it would pour down for weeks, complete with thunder and lightning: there is nothing to compare with a tropical rainstorm. Before then it would get hotter and more uncomfortable. My mother must have hated Lagos at that time of the year, but it obviously hadn't yet occurred to me how strange it must have been for her to eat Christmas pudding in a cotton dress and spend Christmas afternoon on the beach.

I don't remember anything of the flight over. My grandparents met us at Heathrow and my grandfather took me into the washroom and made me put on the sweater and the duffel coat he had brought along. Within a month my mother found a live-in job at a hotel in Cornwall where she went with my sister. I started at the local school, St Leonard's. It was here that I first learnt about cricket, a game that can only be understood in terms of the British temperament: fair play, never argue with the umpire, don't make a fuss even if the other man is cheating. I played for the school. For a long time afterwards I kept the cutting from the local paper with the picture of the team taken after we won a competition. I lost the cutting in Ireland, twelve years later. Nothing else from my childhood survived my return to Britain at sixteen.

Once a month my grandparents took me to visit relatives or to see the sights: the Tower; Madame Tussaud's; St Paul's; the Christmas lights in Regent Street. They were both in their sixties then and I don't suppose they wanted the responsibility of a child all over again, but they were good, decent people who gave me far more than they ever knew. This included, above all, the emotional security which had gone with the breakdown of my parents' marriage when the cultural tensions finally erupted. This was invariably the case in all those marriages unless one or other of the partners subsumed themselves completely in the culture of the other. It was in the nature of these things that both partners were wilful people who had already transgressed powerful barriers merely by getting married.

The tensions lived on in the divided allegiance of the children, who themselves personified divisions within the marriages. Literally so. I am the product of both but, on the outside at least, different from either, hence the plethora of ugly euphemisms used to describe people like me: mixed-race, half-caste, mulatto: the connotations are meant to be demeaning, and so they are. According to the OED, mulatto is defined as 'the offspring of White person and Negro; of colour of mulattos, tawny [f. Sp. *mulato* young mule, mulatto, irreg. f. *mulo* MULE]'; mule is defined as 'the offspring (usu. sterile) of he-ass and mare, or (pop.) of she-ass and stallion (prop. *hinny*), used as beast of draft and burden and undeservedly noted for obstinacy; stupid or obstinate person; hybrid plant or animal.'

If we are to judge human beings in terms of colour alone; if colour does indeed possess the status of an absolute, then I am a hybrid and sterile because I can't reproduce myself, except with another hybrid. I'm not 'pure'. Any child I have will approximate more closely to the colour of its mother, whether white or black; and already, even within the first generation, one or other of the 'races' – as distinct from the human race, to which we all, presumably, belong – will begin to disappear.

But I'm only sterile if colour is indeed an absolute. I'm not sterile in the strictly biological sense. My ability to reproduce another human being is not in question. The resultant child may be white or black but it would be my child. What is in question is my own uncertain status in the colour game, which is the only logical reason for the link between me, the 'offspring of a White person and Negro', and a mule, the 'offspring of he-ass and mare', with the corresponding suggestion that such a union is somehow against nature. And perhaps because this is not grounded in any biological fact, the concept of the unnatural coupling of the two goes beyond biology and assumes a mythic force in the collective consciousness.

This isn't only a European perception, the result of a specifically British – or European – sickness: 'We don't see the colour of our children,' a Nigerian friend said to me once, but she was indulging in a fiction in order to be able to charge the British with racism. A recent book by the present Nigerian ambassador to the United Nations refers disparagingly to the prime minister of a neighbouring country as 'one of those mulatto intellectuals who seem to pop up with alarming regularity in a number of Marxist revolutionary parties in Africa'. The author clearly expects his readers to feel the same sense of mistrust and something not quite right about the creature he's referring to *because* he's a 'mulatto'; and it's obvious that he hasn't thought through the extra-ordinarily undiplomatic implications of what he's written. And in his lack of diplomacy he's unwittingly voiced the related idea of the hybrid as unbalanced, as though the suspicion of racial 'impurity' brought in its wake not only sterility but, being sterile, a spiritual or psychic or emotional imbalance.

Given these attitudes it's hardly any wonder that people like me, mixed-race people (like: mixed fruit and nuts, something you buy in the supermarket), become obsessive about colour and aggressive about identity and sometimes end up rejecting one country in favour of the other. Unfortunately, the question of one's identity can't be posited on the rejection of a parent, which is what this amounts to, and which is the real offence against biology. The demand that a person should make such a choice does not lie within anybody's power, and yet it is a demand which is made every time someone indulges in the semantics of the colour game.

If, according to this language, colour is an absolute; if black and white are absolutely different, and if by this token I'm indeed sterile because I can't reproduce myself, then the biological imperative would seem to presuppose nothing less than the hand of God. So we begin with a lie and before long we find ourselves carrying out the divine will. We enslave one group and gas another and we can do these things with impunity because, according to the language we use and the categories it generates, there is no actual crime involved in ridding the earth of such abominations: these people are different, after all, of another species, and ultimately no different, in terms of perception, from the mule we turn into a beast of burden.

The suspicion of divine intervention and our own role as God's servants accounts, perhaps, for the mythology of the mulatto in the collective imagination – African or European, black or white. This is seen most clearly, and no doubt for good historical reasons, in the literature of the American South. William Faulkner's *Light in August* portrays a man whose 'mixed blood' dictates his isolation from any recognisably human community, such isolation being the condition of the true outsider and not the romantic fantasy of the suburban imagination:

> He did not look like a professional hobo in his professional rags, but there was something definitely rootless about him, as though no town nor city was his, no street, no walls, no square of earth his own.

Joe Christmas is so far outside any of society's conventions, he is so marginal and so alone, that he can kill a human being without conscience. It means nothing to him to take a life because no other life is real for him, including his own. And in the end he must be destroyed because society cannot tolerate what he represents.

But Joe Christmas is white; that is to say, he looks white. It's only later that the people of the town discover that he has black blood; that he's a 'nigger': ' "I said all the time that he wasn't right. Wasn't a white man. That there was something funny about him. But you can't tell folks nothing until – " '.

Part of Faulkner's genius was to explore what we mean by colour when a person looks white but is 'really' black, and to do so by pushing the language of colour to its extreme. If colour means anything then Joe Christmas is white. But Joe Christmas only looks white, even to those who should know: ' "It's a white man," he said, without turning his head, quietly, "What you want, whitefolks?" '

His colour is only a mask, an illusion. Our eyes have deceived us because our language is inaccurate. Joe Christmas's sudden mutation from white to black involves only those who see him. He himself remains the same. Put another way, colour is only the symbol of imagined difference. The mistake is to substitute the symbol for the real thing. When we use the language of colour we're mesmerised by the power of the symbol and we forget that we started by talking about something else.

This is what I gradually began to perceive after my experience with Alan in Wembley, soon after I returned to Britain. When I told myself that colour bored me it was because I knew instinctively that I was being asked to collaborate in a lie in order that others should feel better about the world they had constructed. At the time I didn't have the resources or the experience to follow it through. I could avoid the issue easily enough when I wrote about Nigeria because the special status colour conferred on me within the society reinforced my own ambivalent relationship towards it. Any deeper examination was unnecessary, at least for my immediate purposes.

In Britain, where I am seen as black, my responses are more problematical. Quite how problematical only revealed itself after I had written the first draft of this essay and then understood that if I was to say anything about Britain, about my mother's country and what it means to me, what it continues to mean to me, I would have to deal with the issue directly. And the corollary of this was that I would also have to examine the ways in which I was estranged from this society because of my profound connection with another.

The real tension is cultural. Human beings belong to cultures. The 22-year-old trainee telephone engineer who told me about his visit to Jamaica and his first meeting with his grandmother was British. His connection with Jamaica was accidental, and even less meaningful than the connections which the Canadians I knew had with their ancestral homes. The Canadians needed a more significant relationship with these other cultures because Canada was a new country without the weight and solidity and sheer gravitational pull of an old country like Britain. My own tension is, precisely, the gravity exerted by two immensely powerful cultures.

I'm a hybrid in terms of culture, not colour. Two cultures co-exist within me, neither of which can be reconciled with the other. My colour is merely the outward sign of a profounder dislocation, and of no importance in itself. Similarly, the colour of my child will only reflect the culture to which it belongs – African or European, black or white. My child can only inherit one side of my dual heritage, not both.

This tension needn't have been quite so stark. If I had stayed on with my grandparents when I first came over at eleven I would have been in a position similar to that of the trainee telephone engineer. I might then have visited Nigeria as an adult and I would have seen the dirt and the squalor and the corruption and the inefficiency. I would have seen the 'Third World', and that's all I would have seen.

My grandparents would have helped to make this so. To them the matter was simple. I was their grandchild. My grandmother in particular was going to make an Englishman of me one way or another. I suppose she must have thought I had come to stay, or perhaps she just decided that it was safer for her to work on that assumption. She treated me as if I was wholly British; as if I had been brought up in Britain all along; as if I had no knowledge of another society, of those powerful associations which a place – a street, a wall, a square of earth – holds for us, any reminder of which is enough to break one's heart. But then she knew nothing of Nigeria. She hadn't travelled much. She went to Canada once to visit her older daughter, but even that journey was problematic: my grandfather apparently complained endlessly that he couldn't get proper beer.

Nigeria must have appeared a threatening place to my grandparents, especially in the beginning, when my mother first went out, in the days before popular air travel, when a telephone call had to be booked days in advance. They used to phone us once a year, my mother shouting into the phone to be heard above the crackling as we lined up to wish them Happy Christmas. Later, Nigeria became the place where their daughter was unhappy, and how helpless they must have felt when they first began to hear about her unhappiness. And yet, when Nigeria came to their house in the form of my father, on his way back from a conference in the United States, his eyes red from exhaustion and his suit crumpled from the long flight, my grandmother made sure that I put on a clean shirt – 'You want to look smart for your father' – and my grandfather took him to his local for a pint.

My most poignant memory of the year I lived with my grandparents was coming home from school on a winter's evening – the sharp, acrid smell of smoke on the air; a smell full of associations which still has the power to take me back to that house in Streatham – and telling them that I had been called a 'wog' in the playground. It was a measure of my hurt that I overrode my natural pride and blurted this out; and I knew, even as I spoke, that my grandparents couldn't say anything useful, just as I knew that by presenting it in this way I was only distressing them. Children almost always understand more than adults, who have themselves forgotten much of what they knew when they were children; but if I understood that it would have been better to keep silent, I was only a child after all and unable to exercise that level of emotional control.

My grandfather, a gentle and sensitive man, looked downcast as he pulled on his pipe and gazed at the coal fire that he was forever poking and prodding and complaining at, as though it was a mischievous spirit that had been sent to try him; my grandmother, more combative and more assertive, attempted to hide her own hurt by what she imagined was sound advice: 'Remember, dear, next time they call you that, just tell them the word means "gentleman".' Of course I had no intention of saying anything of the kind, but I promised her I would and I loved her for suggesting such a hopelessly inadequate response. I wonder whether they thought that was the end of the matter. At any rate I never mentioned it again and neither did they.

Strangely enough, this is all that I remember about the incident. I don't remember the circumstance surrounding the name-calling, or whether it ever happened again. I don't even remember the words I used when I told my grandparents, or the inflection in my voice. I only remember the look on my grandfather's face and my grandmother's advice. But memory isn't to be trusted because it is always at the mercy of the will; and because I loved my grandparents; because the year I lived with them was such a happy period for me; and because their country was also my country and I was determined to stake my claim, it may not be strange after all that my childish will should have abolished so effortlessly any sign of rejection. Children can be ruthlessly single-minded because they haven't yet grasped the distance between what they want and what the world will permit them.

As a child in Britain I did many things unconsciously that should have told me a great deal about my sense of Britishness, of which my accent was only the most obvious. It seems extraordinary to me now that I should have learnt to speak with a perfectly unremarkable middle-class English accent. To hear me speak one would never guess that I had lived for any length of time in another country, and yet I had spent the greater part of my childhood in Nigeria. The fact that my mother was British and that English was spoken in our house doesn't sufficiently account for my adopted accent. My father spoke with a strong Nigerian inflection and my mother had a slight but noticeable Scots burr. I perfected my accent during my year in London, under my grandmother's careful guidance; and if she succeeded in making an Englishman of me (even of the hybrid variety) then it was because I collaborated with her in the endeavour.

The deeper question as to why I applied my will in this way is one that I have never been able to adequately answer, unless I somehow knew that it was my fate to live in Britain. If this was the case, if it is indeed true that we are born with the foreknowledge of our destiny, then I acted on this knowledge by ensuring that my accent would never betray me as a foreigner. People respond to what they hear at least as much as they respond to what they see. Foreignness begins, not with colour, but with language, which is why, when people speak with foreigners, they talk slowly and pronounce their words carefully. If I spoke like an Englishman then I was an Englishman.

Meanwhile, the question which has so far been lurking won't go away and needs to be asked: Is Britain a racist society? Do the institutions of the State, those expressions of the popular will – the schools, the police, the House of Commons – discriminate against people on the basis of colour and only colour? The short answer is, I don't know; and nor, probably, does anyone else, although I admired Beryl Bainbridge's honesty in admitting her own confusions and doubts, even if I would have preferred a deeper elucidation of them. But to put the question so crudely is problematical because it may only serve to hide a deeper complexity. I suspect that in so far as the British can be called racist – to the extent that they identify skin colour with inherent difference – they do so out of what might better be called cultural chauvinism.

All cultures are profoundly chauvinistic. It is their single most important defining characteristic, what they are as cultures. In Nigeria, for instance, a Yoruba parent will not take kindly to their child marrying someone from the Hausa north because the Hausas are different: they speak a different language, they wear different clothes, they have different customs. The Yoruba word for the Igbos in the east translates as 'a race of cannibals'. If the Hausas and the Igbos were a different colour we would doubtless call the Yoruba response racist, which it clearly isn't.

Colour, in fact, may only be the convenient shorthand for a much larger concept; and its very obviousness, the ease with which we can identify an immediate visual difference with a profounder difference of what it means to belong to a particular society, may for that reason be misleading. People will always dissemble where they can. This isn't necessarily because human beings are mendacious by nature, though they are that, but because they don't themselves know what they think, and will simplify every time.

Conversely, the British are no less disparaging about foreigners who are the same colour as themselves. Those notorious signs outside rooming houses in the fifties and sixties were directed as much against the Irish as against the 'Coloureds'; and everybody knows that the Germans are 'krauts', the Spanish 'dagos', and the French 'frogs'. I was shocked when I first became aware of anti-Semitism in Britain. Somebody I knew quite well, a university student in those days and possibly now an editor in a London publishing house, referred to a mutual acquaintance of ours as 'that dirty little Jew'. They could say this in front of me since, whatever my faults, I was clearly not Jewish; on the other hand, and for this reason, I'm probably not the best guide to racism in Britain.

There is also the complicating fact of class in British society. From direct experience I know very well that my middle-class accent and my middle-class profession and my middle-class values are more important than my colour. I have seen this in the (significantly) few occasions that I have come into contact with the police. But I know very well that their responses are dictated purely in terms of class, not colour, and that, like all British people, they read every subtle nuance of class with unthinking precision. One has only to observe the way in which foreigners consistently misread the same clues to appreciate how instinctive is the assessment with the British. A name, a hairstyle, a way of walking; each one by itself is sufficient to place a person with a great degree of accuracy. Try explaining this to a foreigner and judge how complex is this business of class; try telling them that the profession and the income and the newspaper are clues but it's more than this, and they might be forgiven for supposing that they were learning about the endless convolutions of the Indian caste system.

The real genius of the class system, the reason why it has survived so well and in such apparent conflict with the democratic and egalitarian values of the modern world – 'we hold these truths to be self-evident, that all men are created equal': but perhaps this is just a New World idea – is because it is maintained by the subtle collusion of everyone who belongs to it. Social systems are dependent wholly on the will of the people who make up that system, unless they are living under a tyranny. In the course of his recent book on Britain, *Coasting,* Jonathan Raban, who toured Britain at the same time as Theroux (but by sea and in the opposite direction), makes the mistake of opening his mouth while on a miners' picket in South Yorkshire:

It was the extraordinary speed of it which was so English. It wasn't my clothes – the Italian truck-load of winter fashionwear had guaranteed that I couldn't possibly look conspicuous on a picket line. It was accent, and nothing but accent. *How far's Rossington* was enough to open the chasm of all the dirty and invidious distinctions of the English class set-up.

It was accent, and nothing but accent: language again, already understood by an eleven-year-old fresh from the colonies. It was all in the way one spoke, to say nothing of the words one used: dinner/lunch; sweet/ pudding; scone/scone. Even now, after eighteen years, I'm sometimes uncertain about the class status of a particular word. This doesn't matter since my own uncertain status – British-but-not-British; a hybrid – permits me a certain latitude. People will overlook the occasional mispronunciation or a word misused because I'm not a threat to their sense of safety in the security of their surroundings.

The outsider may suffer from their marginalisation in the society, but they have a corresponding freedom which is genuinely liberating. I don't have to concern myself with those aspects of British society which I find unproductive. Class is an anachronism which limits lives and prevents communication between people who share a common history and a common destiny. Jonathon Raban's sympathy with the striking miners could never be translated into action because in the eyes of his compatriots he was an Englishman who was even worse than a foreigner: a foreigner-who-was-not-a-foreigner.

It has taken me a long time to understand the depth of the British class system, and longer again to understand how profoundly people identify with their place in it. 'I'm working class and proud of it,' Alan said rather aggressively when I probed him on this during one of our evening strolls. I was bemused at the time. My Yoruba background had told me all that I needed to know about finely graded social hierarchies, but I had also absorbed the get-ahead attitudes of the Nigerian society. The average Nigerian would be appalled to hear those same miners who turned on Raban go on to say that they were fighting for their sons. No Nigerian is about to go down a mine for his son to follow him. If that happened his life would have been a waste; he would have been a failure. The point about going down a mine was for your son to become an engineer.

I didn't properly understand Alan's proud declaration

of allegiance. I didn't listen to him; I only heard the words. So I thought of him as a failure, as I would have considered myself a failure if I had been condemned to remain in that factory in Wembley for the rest of my life. Anyone who did a menial job was a failure. Only a fool would pretend that it was a source of pride and a mark of identity. The failure might have been the result of chance or stupidity or even witchcraft, but it was failure all the same.

It's arguable that the police treat blacks in much the same way that they treat the working-class: to be kept in their place. There are good historical reasons why this should be so, since the majority of British-Caribbeans happen to be working-class: they live in working-class areas, they go to working-class schools, they aspire to working-class jobs. Translated into political terms, they are without power and they are treated as such. And not only blacks, or the working-class, but any group which is similarly powerless. We all saw on our television screens the ugly scenes of the police breaking up perfectly peaceful hippie convoys on their way to Stonehenge for the summer solstice.

No doubt individual policemen are racist in the crude sense that their responses to people of a different colour are irrational, but the world is full of people whose responses are just as irrational towards those who worship a different god or speak a different language or eat different food. Human beings are irrational, which is why they express themselves so badly when they are called upon to explain their strange behaviour. 'I don't like blacks' is a nonsense statement because it doesn't mean anything; and it is for this reason that a racist joke can be told in front of a black who is 'one of us, not like them', because at that moment the black is not 'seen' as black, and in a way which very much matters he isn't black.

What *is* depressing is that the racial hatred perpetrated by a minority has been, if not tacitly condoned,
then wilfully neglected. This is a typically British
attitude which is sometimes misread as hypocrisy.
When I lived in Lewes, an archetypal English county
town not far from the National Front headquarters in
Brighton, I came across a group of NF activists selling
their broadsheet outside the law courts on the High
Street. Nobody paid them the least attention, not even
my middle-class neighbours with their 'I'm against
racism' stickers on the front windows of their houses
and the rear windows of their Volvos: why is the English
middle-class so tirelessly conformist?

There is a maddening streak of complacency in the
British which is the reverse of their sense of safety in
their surroundings. They cannot be easily threatened,
and so they are unable to grasp the levels of anger,
frustration and fear that is the legacy of those whose
connection with the society is tenuous and uncertain.
Immigrants are always vulnerable if only because they
aren't equipped to decode the signals but are anxious
not to misread them. Never mind that the signals may
not need close reading: it only takes one stone through
your window, one obscenity scrawled on your wall, one
verbal threat to your child, for the outsider to panic.

And for good reason. Consider the recent events in a
primary school in the otherwise nondescript town of
Dewsbury, near Bradford, where twenty-six white
children were kept at home by their parents because
their local school, Headfield, was predominantly Asian.
The parents claimed that such a high proportion of
Asian children – eighty-five per cent of the total –
jeopardised their own children's educational standards
by putting excessive emphasis on Asian culture in a
country where this was redundant, such as studying

Urdu and learning about Islam. Nine months later the matter had still not been resolved and the twenty-six children were attending classes run by a retired headmaster in a room above a pub.

Matters weren't helped at the time this first blew up when the National Front promptly joined the bandwagon and attempted to organise a march through the town centre; and a prominent member of the British aristocracy, whose much-touted views include repatriation of the entire immigrant population as the only 'peaceful solution' to all of Britain's problems – including, presumably, soccer hooliganism – rushed up from her well-appointed London home to give the beleaguered parents the benefit of her advice. The issue was quickly taken up in the pages of the *Star*, where a journalist known as 'the Angry Voice' gave us his considered opinion:

There are only two questions to be asked about the 26 children who are being denied entry to Overthorpe school, even though there is room for them.

The first question is this: Would you send *your* child to a predominantly white school, or to another school which is over-whelmingly Asian?

If you are white, then there is only one obvious answer – even though it begs the second question: Is it racist to think like this?

The answer to this is clear: Of course it is racist, and the parents should not be ashamed of admitting it.

They are also right to want the best for their children, and the best cannot be an education at

an English school where most of the pupils don't
even have English as their first language.

And Asian children, particularly: this obsessive hatred
of people from the Indian subcontinent is paralleled in
recent history by a well-known event in central Europe.
Around the time of the Dewsbury fiasco there happened
to be a military coup in Fiji. The Angry Voice, ever
vigilant, always ready to defend to the death if necessary the purity of a mongrel race – Saxon, Viking, Celt,
Huguenot, African, Asian; 'And here begins the
Ancient Pedigree/ That so exalts our Poor Nobility:/
'Tis that from some *French* Trooper they derive,/ Who
with the *Norman* Bastard did arrive. . . ,' in Defoe's
words – fires off a broadside which somehow manages to
return to his favourite theme:

> The natives are revolting in Fiji because
> immigrant Indians now outnumber them and
> have taken power. Given that Britain's Asians
> are multiplying disturbingly faster than the
> national average – and that's a fact – how much
> longer before it happens here?

Breeding like rabbits, I daresay; but the ease with which
this sort of language is tolerated is depressing in the
extreme. And full marks to the *Socialist Worker* for
their insistence that 'the saddest aspect of the
Dewsbury row is how organised racists have exploited
the fears of ordinary working class people', even if they
also indulge in the convenient – and insulting – left-

wing fiction that the British working-class is inherently decent by virtue of being working-class.

Leaving aside the inconvenient fact of the *Star's* actual readership, which is certainly not middle-class, it is never the case that an accident of birth, which dictates many things, including where you live and what you eat and how well your children are educated, also dictates the moral judgments an individual human being will make in the course of their life. It certainly doesn't dictate the behaviour of an entire class; that same class, incidentally, which marched against blacks in 1948 in order to keep British-Caribbean seamen off British ships; or that same class which, with the full support of the Transport and General Workers' Union, banned overtime on the buses in Wolverhampton in 1955 'as a protest against the increasing number of coloured workers employed'.

I don't think that this particular hornet's nest need be disturbed, particularly not in the patronising support of a romanticised middle-class notion concerning the virtues of their working-class brethren. The ability to be a moral human being has nothing to do with class or colour or any of the other artificial attributes we assign to one another in order to simplify the universe, but to what an individual human being is on the (mercifully few) occasions they are called upon to make profound moral judgments.

But perhaps we can dismiss the angry voice on the grounds that what he believes is only read by the powerless and who cares what they think as long as they aren't in a position to subvert the institutions of the State for their own ends? Perhaps; though it would be hard to convince an Asian family in a tower block whose lives are made a daily misery by the antics of some members of the *Star's* readership. Any lie is dangerous;

in a highly literate culture the written lie is the most dangerous of all. But what is one supposed to think when these same ideas of racial intolerance are given a bogus intellectualism by people who hold influential posts in the academic world and who write for publications which are read by people who do very much matter, by the people who, directly or otherwise, control these same institutions of the State?

John Casey is a fellow of Caius College, Cambridge, and co-founder of the Conservative Philosophy Group. In the Autumn 1982 issue of the *Salisbury Review*, a 'quarterly magazine of Conservative thought', he published an article called 'One Nation: The Politics of Race'. This article is worth examining in some detail as an example of what happens when we take the language of colour to its logical end.

Casey begins by quoting Burke on what it means to belong to a nation or a society, both concepts for his purposes being interchangeable, and both suggesting the idea of continuity in time and space: a nation or a society is an organic growth, and not to be understood '*speculatively*: for instance, by invoking alleged universal principles like "the rights of man", principles which are taken to transcend the customs, pieties, traditions of a particular nation – of *this* nation'.

England, then – but not Britain – is a discrete nation or society by virtue of its own particular history, and part of that history includes an intellectual tradition which embraces not only Burke but also Coleridge, Matthew Arnold, Newman, Ruskin, William Morris and T. S. Eliot. These names are not mentioned, he assures us, 'because I want to appeal to authority', but because 'I wish to point a contrast'. That is to say, there is a deep and profound connection 'between the culture of a community and its sense of itself as a nation', a connection which has been betrayed in the language of modern politics, but which nevertheless exists at a level inseparable one from the other: England *is* its intellectual tradition, and it is out of this tradition that its unique political institutions exist.

From this general introduction Casey then moves on to consider two particular cases, Northern Ireland and the Falkland Islands, in order to elucidate his argument. In the case of the former, the justification for the continued British presence is not based simply on the fact that the majority of the people in the six counties want to be British – 'That the wish of the majority of the Northern Irish to remain British should be respected must depend upon facts beyond the mere existence of such a wish' – but that the majority who so wish it has lived there a long time:

> In other words their wish to remain British
> commands respect because they *are* British, a
> fact which discloses itself through the occasions,
> tempers, dispositions and moral and special
> habitudes of the people, only in a long space of
> time.

Sentiment, then – the wish – is not enough in itself for a people to be considered to belong to a particular nation or society; it certainly isn't enough to justify the presence of British troops on alien soil. This is a clear enough statement, if somewhat problematical: what constitutes a sufficient length of time, and who decides on the precise figure, are conveniently overlooked. But no matter; we already know that those who seek to corner the high ground in the moral debate always begin by defining the limits of the discourse.

The case for considering the Falkland Islanders to be also British is less clear, and involves a contradiction, as follows: the justification for the Falklands war lies in the fact that 'the Falklands were sovereign territory, perhaps strategically important, and that the Falklanders were *British* by every conceivable test, by language, custom and race'. In other words, as Casey goes on, 'nationality, in addition to whatever else it may be, is a *sentiment*. It cannot be *reduced* to such things as long settlement in one place, legal and constitutional continuity, shared religion and culture, because all these things may exist without the sentiment of nationality.'

So what is it to be then? We have one argument for Northern Ireland and another for the Falkland Islands. But let us not allow ourselves to be distracted, even by the contradiction of a professional philosopher. We shall return to this in due course. In the meantime, there is more to come, and it is worse.

The reason behind all this talk of 'sentiment' and 'fact' is to prepare the way for the central thesis of the article, which is the 'problem' of the 'West Indians' in British – or English – society, even those who were born here, even those who have never set foot on West Indian soil, even those who are *not West Indian*.

The 'sentiments' which exclude them from the honour of being considered English are reduced to a number of unsupported statements: 'they' resent authority, including 'the police, teachers, Underground guards'; 'they' have a different family structure 'which is markedly unlike our own'; 'they' are intellectually backward, 'below those of all other racial groups'; and 'they' have a propensity towards criminal activity, arson apparently being their speciality owing to their 'curious interest in fire'. This is an impressive list, and nowhere substantiated. In which ways do their family structures differ? On what grounds does he claim that they lean towards criminal behaviour? Who says that they are less intelligent? For a man who himself leans so heavily on authority these are telling omissions; and his beloved Burke, whose words he quotes but whose spirit he betrays, would have been more rigorous:

It is therefore our business carefully to cultivate in our minds, to rear to the most perfect vigour and maturity, every sort of generous and honest feeling that belongs to our nature. To bring the dispositions that are lovely in private life into the service and conduct of the common wealth; so to be patriots, as not to forget we are gentlemen.

But, of course, the truth of the matter has nothing to do with sentiments or facts, or with Burke for that matter, but with colour. We should have been alerted by the early use of the word 'race' (that misnomer again), so deftly slipped in when he was discussing the Britishness of the Falkland Islanders.

The British-Caribbeans are an altogether different case. Why?:

Because of their sudden and recent entry, because they are already a very large community, but above all because of their colour, which distinguishes them from the rest of the

> population in both their own eyes and others' eyes,
> they have a solidarity one with another that gives
> them a sense of identity and interest [arson?]
> different (in their eyes) from that of the majority.

This is a very weak argument indeed for a mind so highly trained: if they are different because they share a sense of identity based on their perception of their difference from the rest of the society, this difference being reduced to colour alone, then it would only take a sufficient number of them to refuse to share the perception for Casey's argument to collapse. A simple referendum will do, except that the answer may not be to his liking.

But is our professor trying to provide himself with a loophole; as if to say, we think they're different but that's OK because they do too? Whatever one's doubts about Caryl Phillips's book, *The European Tribe*, the point about the incidents with the teacher at school and the editor in the publishing house was not that *he* felt different, but that *they* made him feel different. This, precisely, was the problem.

. . . but above all because of their colour, Casey says, and this is where we have been heading all along; this is the end result of Burke and Coleridge and Matthew Arnold and all that elevated talk of sentiment and fact. Colour, nowhere mentioned in the case of Northern Ireland or the Falklands, has swept all else aside: it is enough that 'they' are black, unlike the Northern Irish or the Falkland Islanders, who, presumably, are white; and in no time at all the barbarians are at the gates:

> . . . I do not wish to say that the problem about

the West Indian community is just about the possible destruction of civilised life in the centres of the big cities. (Although this is what is happening.) It is also that all this offends a sentiment – a sense of what English life should be like, of how the English behave towards duly constituted authority, a sense of what is civilised behaviour.

Thus the riots of 1981 – but what else can one expect from savages? – despite what the *'bien pensant* sociologists'* say to the contrary. *We* will say nothing of the scenes we witness every Saturday afternoon at football clubs up and down the country involving white (civilised?) Englishmen. No, the two are not the same, but it would be fruitless arguing that whereas the explosions of 1981 were the result of certain kinds of thought processes; that they were in fact the consequences of bigotry, the football hooliganism perpetrated every week by 'true' Englishmen, by the descendants of Newman, Ruskin and William Morris, is the behaviour of the real barbarians. However, barbarians occur at all times and in all societies: the barbarians you will always have with you, and in every colour under the sun.

What do we say of someone who sees colour, and only colour, and who imagines, or wants to imagine, that this perception is grounded in fact, is not a subjective judgment but has an objective (measurable) corollary? Because the English are 'white', a second or third generation 'black' can never be English but must always remain 'West Indian', in exactly the same way that the Jew in Nazi Germany could never be a German, Germans being, by definition, not-Jews. And the racist would, presumably, if pushed, begin to define degrees of blackness: when is black black? One-quarter; one eighth; one sixteenth? Shall we talk of quadroons and octoroons and the thirty-two shades of colour which operated under French colonial society?

I'm sure that John Casey would want to distance himself from the terrifying implications of his own argument, an argument which dispenses with morality in the ordinary sense of the term and leaves the way open to all manner of things. Without the notion of 'rights' in the abstract ('alleged universal principles') the very idea of human beings as moral agents, as possessing the ability to act for good or evil, is repugnant to him: 'it would clearly be morally indefensible to send men to their deaths in defence of a *principle*, rather than of sovereign territory or national interest,' he says of the Falklands conflict.

The only morality lies in this dubious business of nationhood, but only as defined by him:

The 'sentiment' of nationality is actually one's ability to see the community in which one lives, and to see that as a moral idea.

This is pretentious: the State can do no wrong; the State is permitted, by virtue of being the State, to do anything at all. It is a chilling formulation because we know very well the consequences of such a 'philosophy' if carried to an appalling extreme: a universe which considers true moral action 'morally indefensible' is helpless against evil; must, presumably, remain silent as millions of human beings are annihilated and buried in mass graves, or herded into townships and slowly exterminated by death squads.

How much blood must spill in our blood-soaked

century, how many human beings – God's children, all
of them, whatever their colour or shape or language or
custom or nation – must be brutalised by the almighty
State before we dispense with all this talk of 'them' and
'us' and remember that we are all each other's flesh?

Still, John Casey's argument doesn't need to consider
anything as drastic as the above examples of modern
history. Britain in the 1980s is a long way from
Germany in the 1930s and this is largely because the
horror of Nazism continues to inform the European
imagination at the most potent level. Even the idea of
repatriation needs to be articulated carefully, hence the
defensive note of those who seek to recommend it. Casey
writes:

> At the centre of the moral and emotional
> objection to even *considering* any large-scale
> repatriation of coloured immigrants – by
> whatever means, however financially
> advantageous – stands the idea that they are
> 'black Englishmen'. This is a notion that trades
> upon the idea of Englishness whilst at the same
> time taking away those very features that give it
> emotional weight. Had the immigrant community
> been here fifty, eighty, a hundred years, it would
> look more and more as though it were composed
> of Black Englishmen. This would be still more
> clearly true if it adopted the culture, customs and
> values of the English. But at the moment it looks
> much more likely that the large, self-conscious
> black and brown communities will turn Britain
> itself into a different sort of place.

*

Anyone who objects to repatriation, then, any Englishman, that is – women being entirely peripheral, to say
nothing of the Scots and the Welsh and the Cornish – not
only invites the destruction of civilisation-as-we-know-
it by the hordes in our midst, but, infinitely worse,
offends against a moral idea (nationhood) and betrays
his inherited tradition, what he very much is as an
Englishman. Any such objection, in fact, would be
positively unpatriotic; and when a person abrogates for
themselves the sole right to define what constitutes
patriotism in a given society then we have legitimate
reason to be worried. One would have hoped, at this late
hour, that the twentieth-century worship of the State
(how many millions dead?) would have cured us for ever
of this disease. Evidently not: it would seem that this
god demands even more blood.

And, yet, the defensive note remains, so much so that
any argument in favour of repatriation must somehow
suggest that those who find it shocking – the victims
apart – are simply deluding themselves for reasons
which remain obscure:

> . . . many people envisage, with regret certainly,
> but not with *horror*, that a large proportion of
> Whites will, in a few years, leave Zimbabwe for
> Britain and South Africa . . . Their possible
> departure is looked upon as something that can
> be negotiated about by Britain for the best
> possible terms but not as a nameless horror.

In fact this is not true. Those whites who chose to leave
Zimbabwe did so because they, too, had parcelled the
world according to colour, had raised colour above all

else, and had for that reason, and only that reason, prolonged a long and bloody civil war; and even Casey must be aware that the new government of the independent country asked those same whites to stay behind and help build the new State. But why does Casey use this example? How does the position of whites in one country bear on the position of the blacks in another? Repatriation is not an issue in Zimbabwe.

Casey knows very well that any talk of repatriation would be vehemently opposed by 'the liberal consensus', by the well-meaning but misguided people who eat brown rice and vote Labour and live in Camden Town, which is why he is quick to acknowledge that the resultant furore 'could actually lead to illegal and offensive pressure upon immigrants of a sort that it is of overwhelming importance to avoid'. Why one should actually care about public opinion in an amoral universe in unclear, but boldness and audacity are not among the more prominent qualities of Casey's argument. His answer, retrospective legislation, which would 'alter the legal status of the coloured immigrant community, so that its members became guest-workers . . .' – and how smart the Germans turned out to be concerning their Turkish garbage collectors! – is typical of the unease which he himself feels:

We can well imagine the outcry that there would be both at home and abroad. However, this policy would have about it an air of inevitability once enacted, and of political control that might actually make it less damaging and less inhumane than a voluntary scheme.

*

I don't understand how 'retrospective legislation' (an abhorrent concept) is supposed to alter the effect of an action. And 'less damaging', 'less inhumane' for whom? For the people who are the objects of this action? Or for those who support it? And, for that matter, where are these people to be sent? Why must it be assumed that Jamaica or Barbados or St Lucia would be willing to accept an influx of foreigners for no better reason than that these foreigners happen to be black and therefore unwanted in the country of their birth?

Or perhaps John Casey doesn't realise that two out of every three British-Caribbean people walking the streets and drinking in the pubs and paying their mortgages were born here? I'm not even talking about people like Dave but those who, *by every conceivable test,* including 'culture, customs and values', are citizens of this country and of no other. A strict parallel would be to argue for the repatriation of the descendants of the German immigrants who fled to this country to escape the Nazi terror, but nobody is about to do so. Why? Because they're white. So much for logic; so much for language.

The difference between the *Salisbury Review* and the *Star* is the difference between an academic journal which can quote Burke and a popular newspaper which would not quote Burke as a matter of pride. At bottom, both are saying exactly the same. Once you strip away the contortions of language, once you dispose of all the fanciful theories which contradict each other even as they are being set up, you are left with a series of dubious assertions. To debase another is to debase oneself because – and this is a moral idea: human beings are moral agents or they are nothing – we can only impose suffering when we deny the knowledge of it in ourselves, an act of wilful murder of our most precious inheritance. If this is not so then anything is permitted, including the murder of John Casey for no better reason than that I disagree with him.

Roger Scruton, the editor of the *Salisbury Review* – and also, incidentally, a professional philosopher (O.E.D.: 'A lover of wisdom') – is appalled by the flak John Casey has received at the hands of others for his 'now notorious contribution'. I am in turn appalled that Roger Scruton should imagine that Casey's argument is not misguided: 'And it is in everyone's interest', he writes, 'that people should entertain, in a spirit of free enquiry, opinions which others regard as outrageous, in order that the truth should at last be known.'

On what grounds, for instance – and to take one extreme example – would Scruton justify the publication of an article by Roy Kerridge, entitled 'Black Theology'? Consider the following:

If a generalisation can be made about the Soul of a People, then the West African soul and that of new world Negroes has, in its innermost midst, a core of Terror. Terror originally of the dread forests at night and the spirits in them, then of more tangible threats from slave raiders or the tribe next door, but always the tiny voice of Terror.

I'm hard-pressed to conjure up the image of perfectly normal *British* families on their way to church in London being obscurely driven by what Kerridge imagines to be the racial memory with which he would invest them – the West African forest and so on. This may be my own failure of imagination; it may even be my own suppressed Terror:

> When everything is going well, and no physical
> enemy is present, then invisible evil spirits take
> over the Reign of Terror. Where Negroes live for
> the first time side by side with white people, they
> may regard the latter with timidity or suppressed
> Terror. I rejoice to see this attitude diminishing
> in England and America, but it is still there.

The other day I saw a black family – father, mother, two children – enjoying a day out on the beach at Southend. It was a bank holiday, the first hot day of early summer, and I suddenly found them a tremendously moving sight because I understood something of the courage involved, the simple determination to be just another ordinary British family doing what many ordinary British families do on a hot bank holiday Monday. That courage was marked on their faces and in the way they held themselves and the manner in which they spoke to each other.

One even hesitates to say that they were on holiday. There was nothing carefree about their demeanour. They couldn't enjoy the sun and the sea and the big dipper for their own sakes but as intermittent pleasures to be snatched between the constant and oppressive awareness of other people's perceptions. They were watchful, conspiratorial and quick to detect the first sign of trouble. This in itself created further problems. It is just this self-consciousness which attracts the very attention you shun. If there's one thing that people see it's fear, in the way that animals are supposed to.

Fear brings out the bully in the crowd; the crowd, in turn, may at any moment conjure up the instrument of its chilling vengeance. The yob, the football hooligan, the lager lout: these aren't individual sensibilities which have gone astray because they were unloved as little sensibilities but the creation of all that is dark and hidden in the mass. I don't go to football matches and I rarely drink in pubs for that reason. It isn't worth the hassle. But these are small inconveniences which concern only me. I'm sure that the parents on the beach would rather have foregone their annual holiday than pay for the privilege of their purgatory but for the sake of their children. They wanted to give their children a holiday, and they did, and I admired them for it. I thought they were strong and brave and good people and I would have told them so if it had been possible, but I think the father understood when we glanced at each other as I walked past.

Afterwards, remembering that family as I was writing this essay and trying to understand how they fitted into the narrative, I thought about 'the Angry Voice' and John Casey and Roy Kerridge – those true-blooded Englishmen – and all the nonsense about race and colour, about who belongs and who doesn't belong and how we should define the degrees of belonging suddenly seemed so tiresome. Stupidly, I wished that I could have shown them this perfectly unremarkable sight: stupidly, because they wouldn't have seen what I saw; because it would have been impossible for me to have made them see; because they would have merely looked through their suffocating layers of colour-consciousness, the whole dead weight of unnecessary baggage which ends up splitting families and destroying lives.

We are back again with this problem of seeing: not black lives or white lives or yellow or blue lives but individual human lives, each one more precious than it is possible to say. If the outsider doesn't see the world around them this is partly because the reverse is also true: that world doesn't see them. Dave didn't see trees; John Casey doesn't see people: to Dave, all trees looked the same; to Casey, all blacks look the same. And since Dave knew that, as a human being, he was effectively invisible to John Casey; and since he also knew that his invisibility was a condition which had been imposed upon him but for which he couldn't himself be held responsible, his answer was to render the society itself invisible. It was no longer of any concern to him. At best his relationship with the society was negative. He expected the worst, which is why he could buy a tabloid that recommended his repatriation. He was only interested in the racing tips and the TV programmes.

But the problem with Dave's brand of nihilism, which is what it amounts to, is that it isn't among our possibilities as human beings. One is always obliged to concern oneself with the lies in which people indulge because one can't humanly do anything else. One might otherwise be dead. Dave was dead. He had abrogated the responsibility that the family on the beach confronted every morning when they stepped out of their bed-and-breakfast and took a stroll on the beach. That family asserted life and celebrated it.

I know that John Casey will disagree with me; I know that he will regard what I've just written as another tiresome moral idea calculated to please the liberal sociologists who have betrayed a higher idea of nationhood – not to say England. But I don't think that Casey's article has very much to do with that much-abused word, truth, even if I have no desire to stop him saying what he wants. I'm all for him having his say, although I might wish that the institution which employs him would prove its claim to greatness by distancing itself from such ideas.

Such opinions as Casey possesses can never be coherent. Equally, I have never been impressed with the popular liberal sentiment – and very much a European idea – that one ought to defend to the death a person's right to speak as they wish, which strikes me as just plain silly. Such a view can only be voiced from a position of privilege and power; the person who voices it has never been threatened, and cannot conceive what it is like to live under conditions of siege when the barbarians – the real barbarians, that is, complete with Union Jack T-shirts and tattooed swastikas and cries of 'England, England' – may at any moment threaten your life.

This is not hysteria, still less a manifestation of the slave raid or the West African bush or whatever it is that Roy Kerridge imagines to reside in the collective unconscious, the inheritance no doubt of my Nigerian (tribal?) ancestry. I can assure him that if the night fills me with dread it isn't because I think that the spirits or the slave raiders or the bogeymen are coming to get me, but because I'm all too aware of certain people's questionable sentiments. I am terrified by the perversions of human beings; I am terrified by what they think because the thoughts they have kill people.

In September 1986, a thirteen-year-old British-Asian boy, Ahmed Ullah, was stabbed to death by a fellow pupil at Burnage High School in Manchester. A subsequent report commissioned by Manchester City Council, only parts of which have yet been published, called attention to numerous examples of racist behaviour by some members of staff at the school.

According to an article in the *Independent,* which summarised the uncensored parts of the report:

> A teacher employed specifically to deal with the ethnic minority children being asked by a colleague if her hair-slide was West Indian. 'No,' she replied, 'it's just a hair-slide.' 'Why don't you take that one out and wear it through your nose,' the colleague said.
>
> One teacher speaking to the headmaster about children from ethnic minority backgrounds said: 'I don't like them, they smell.'
>
> Some teachers made blatantly racist remarks, comments which included 'you are like a cartload of monkeys', 'you are not fit to pray' . . . The most common racist remark was to refer to Asian boys as Pakis, sometimes to their faces.

And so on.

In the meantime, a child is dead, killed by another child in the playground of a school in Manchester. But one can hardly accuse a child of murder at any but the most pedantic level. The child who wielded the knife, and whose own life in turn has been destroyed, was only the unwitting agent of lies perpetrated by educated men and women. You don't have to enter the darkness of the West African bush to find the Devil; the Devil can be seen – forked tongue, tail and all – stalking the playground even of Manchester schools in broad daylight.

*

The tendency to play intellectual games with people's lives while deriding deeply felt and often (for that reason) badly articulated truths, is one of the nastier features of the 'race' issue among the Right in this country. This is nowhere more evident than in the current debate on multi-cultural education in a country which has had to absorb a relatively sizable proportion of immigrants from radically different societies.

Consider the case of Ray Honeyford, the former headmaster of Drummond Middle School in Bradford which counted among its pupils a high percentage of children from Asian households. The parents of these children are not themselves British. The overwhelming majority of them are from Pakistan. They came over in the sixties and seventies to work in the woollen mills at a time of labour shortage and have since settled here. And it is their children, first-generation British-Asian children, who are now swelling the school registers. Their background already gives them an entire panoply of different allegiances – language, religion, familial relations – which makes their position far more attenuated than that of the British-Caribbeans, who at least begin with a common language and a common religion.

In 1984 Ray Honeyford published an article in the *Salisbury Review*, in which he voiced his misgivings about conducting lessons in Urdu and substituting the poetry of Linton Kwesi Johnson for that of Shakespeare and Wordsworth. The choice of a British-Caribbean poet in this instance is entirely unhelpful since it conveniently conflates the position of two communities, British-Caribbean and British-Asian, with vastly different experiences as though their positions were identical. This conflation is itself part of the problem of the race issue; and when Honeyford complains, in the

91

course of his article, that the misuse of language by the proponents of multi-culturalism has only obscured the issue by making 'open' and 'honest' discussion impossible, he fails to understand that he has himself already fallen into the same trap.

Honeyford cannot understand why these children, who he says are British children before they are anything else, 'should begin their mastery of English by being taught in Urdu' simply because this is the language of their parents and the one they happen to know best when they enter school. In Honeyford's view – and in this at least he is absolutely right – they are not served by an education which encourages them to think of themselves as anything other than British. As with language, so with religion: Honeyford complains about 'the Muslim parent's insistence on banning his daughter from drama, dance and sport, i.e. imposing a purdah mentality in schools committed to the principle of sexual equality'. An education which is geared towards emphasising their difference only compounds the problem, that of their double allegiance, and ends up producing 'Asian ghettoes'.

These are indeed serious matters, and Honeyford is also right to insist that the children aren't helped by the way in which the debate has largely been hijacked by Left-leaning ideologues whose motives are almost always dishonest, having more to do with 'professional opportunism than the educational progress of ethnic minority children'. And he is right again to accuse certain sections of the immigrant community itself – British-Asian as well as British-Caribbean – of distorting the nature of the problem by retreating into empty slogans for the sake of the political capital.

Honeyford could have added, *apropos* the immigrants themselves, that they might be guilty of using the race issue as an inadequate if understandable way of dealing with their own extremely complex responses.

Human beings cannot be divorced from the culture which produced them: they are that culture or they are nothing. Nowhere does Honeyford even suggest that he has considered what it must mean for a parent to watch their children become strangers to them, still less the courage and the vision, rare enough anywhere, that would be needed for a parent to actively encourage this separation for the sake of the child's well-being in the new society. No immigrant group, as a group, has anywhere ever done this and they aren't ever likely to either. The British themselves are notoriously bad at mixing with the locals when they live in foreign countries, and everybody knows that they take a positive pride in their inability to speak foreign languages.

Nowhere, in fact, is the concept of the foreigner more deeply rooted than here in Britain, which is probably why the regular influx of immigrants into this country has always been its salvation. Civilisations, like human beings, are never static: they must continually be challenged by new ways of looking at the world. The test of a civilisation – and it may even be the definition of one – is its ability to respond to new ideas and new ways of looking at the world. Without this challenge they wither and die. The genius of the British lies in the fact that they know instinctively when they need the input; their obtuseness lies in the way they resist it when it happens. But perhaps this resistance is inevitable; perhaps we always fight against those things which challenge us most profoundly.

Honeyford reproduces a telling passage from a much-quoted book by Chris Mullard, a lecturer in Education at London University, as evidence of the kind of thinking he identifies as typical of the multi-cultural lobby:

> Already we have started to rebel, to kick out against our jailers . . . As more and more black Britons leave school disgruntled, as more black immigrants discard their yoke of humility, the ultimate confrontation will become clearer . . . Blacks will fight with pressure, leaflets, campaigns, demonstrations, fists and scorching resentment which, when peaceful means fail, will explode into street fighting, urban guerrilla warfare, looting, burning and rioting.

Perhaps Mr Mullard has since had reason to doubt the wisdom of this outburst; but in using this passage for his own purposes Honeyford weakens his case by over-stating it. If you disagree with an argument it is more honest and more fruitful to engage with the most articulate expression of it, not the worst, unless you are only interested in sniggering. There is nothing easier than to unearth such a passage in order simply to bury it deeper. And in the process Honeyford pretends amaze-ment that so sensitive an issue should lend itself so easily to hysteria: one may as well refute an 'editorial' in a tabloid than an article in the *Salisbury Review*.

Worse still, Honeyford himself promptly falls into the same trap as Mr Mullard, which only serves to defeat his own purpose. Much has already been made of his own unfortunate outburst against 'The hysterical political temperament of the Indian sub-continent' – so much hysteria! – when, in the course of a parents' evening he had organised to discuss the problem in his school, tempers boiled over. But this is hardly the kind of insult that is designed to help anybody's cause, especially when he goes on to compound his indelicacy by referring to 'A half-educated and volatile Sikh' who 'usurped the privileges of the chair by deciding who was to speak'. He ends by describing Pakistan as 'a country which cannot cope with democracy'; where corruption is endemic; and which 'is the heroin capital of the world'.

These charges may or may not be true, but they are hardly part of his brief: he didn't set out to write a monograph on Pakistan. And perhaps, given the fact of these sentiments and their inclusion in his article, the 'half-educated Sikh' was not so uneducated after all; perhaps he knew exactly what Honeyford thought of him. And not only him, or his sub-continent. The West Indians, it turns out, fare no better.

We will leave aside the insensitive and naive decision to publish in a journal whose politics (or attitudes?) were bound to raise the hackles of the parents who had entrusted their children to his care, and ask instead why the ghost of John Casey should raise itself in the mysterious and wholly unfounded idea that British-Caribbean homes encourage sub-academic offspring:

It is no more than common sense [Honeyford
writes] that if a school contains a
disproportionate number of children . . . from
homes where educational ambition and the
values to support it are conspicuously absent (i.e.
the vast majority of West Indian homes – a
disproportionate number of which are fatherless)
then academic standards are bound to suffer.

*

Truly, Ray Honeyford does not help his own case, and it is a little sad that he seems oblivious of the fact that the journal which was 'fearless' enough to publish his soul-searching article ('I see what I've written as robust and honest rather than wishing to offend. I wanted to get away from the stilted priggishness of the race relations lobby, which inhibits dialogue across the racial boundaries'), was also happy enough to use him for its own political ends. Tell a child that they're a bastard before you know anything about them or their family background and judge whether their response can ever be termed 'stilted priggishness'; tell them repeatedly that they'll never make it in the educational rat-race and then sit back and wonder why they fail their examinations.

Of Roger Scruton, Honeyford has been quoted as saying that 'he's the most intelligent man I've ever met'; but this intelligent man has himself conceded that certain points in Honeyford's article were unfortunate. Perhaps this is an instance of the famous British understatement – a point of pride to the British, after all: plain men who speak plain English – but if Ray Honeyford was merely tactless then Roger Scruton is indeed disingenuous.

Ray Honeyford complains, eleswhere, that the political Right is automatically put on the defensive in any discussion of race because it has to contend 'with the burden of imputed guilt'; and adds: 'The shadows of fascism, the holocaust and apartheid fall across all conservatives who attempt to debate ethnicity.' Quite so; the charge is indeed true, as Honeyford obligingly proves in his own article, and as the *Salisbury Review* proves with monotonous regularity. Again and again Honeyford weakens his case with blanket statements. For instance, those British-Caribbeans Honeyford so loudly denounces are described by him as 'An influential group of black intellectuals of aggressive disposition, who know little of the British traditions of understatement [?], civilised discourse and respect for reason.'

Perhaps these 'black intellectuals' have good reason to doubt the (by now tiresome) notion of civilised British traditions; perhaps Honeyford himself would be similarly aggressive if he had come to this country in good faith only to be met with bigotry and abuse – however understated. God forbid that he should ever wander the streets of an alien city and be denied a bed for the night because his skin was a different colour, or be given – grudgingly – the most menial of jobs because nobody ever imagined that he could do better.

Can it be that Honeyford really fails to understand what happens to children who are daily forced to see their parents humiliated, to be called nigger and wog and sambo, to have shit forced through their letterboxes, and to be told, as Honeyford does repeatedly, that whatever they produce is worthless, of no account, fit only to be sneered at? Why does he never say anything positive? Why are British-Caribbeans only spoken of as hooligans ('violent thugs' in his phrase) whose culture consists solely of creating 'an ear-splitting cacophony for most of the night'? Even their poetry must be ridiculed.

Honeyford betrays his Little Englander mentality in the way in which he uses the example of Linton Kwesi Johnson, four lines of one of whose better-known poems, 'Inglan' is a Bitch', he quotes in support of his argument. Whether or not you like Johnson's work, the man is British and there is absolutely no reason why he shouldn't be studied in schools alongside William Golding, say, or Ted Hughes. Or are they all too contemporary for Honeyford's comfort? Is he one of those people who, had he been born in Wordsworth's day, would have dismissed the great poet for breaking with the glorious tradition and writing in the language of common speech? Johnson, who is 'black', not to say 'West Indian', doesn't even write 'proper' English:

> We in the schools are also enjoined to believe that creole, pidgin other non-standard variants have the same power, subtlety and capacity for expressing five shades of meaning, and for tolerating uncertainty, ambiguity and irony as standard English.

I'm sure that the Scots will have something to say about this, if we take it that Honeyford is also willing to dismiss Robert Burns and Hugh MacDairmid by the very same criterion. And perhaps he is; perhaps Honeyford was one of those people who railed against Tony Harrison for using expletives and Yorkshire dialect in his poems; perhaps Honeyford is one of those Englishmen whose own sense of security in the safety of their surroundings is wholly dependent on received notions of what constitutes the English tradition: Wordsworth is a great poet because everybody has been saying so for the last two hundred years.

As with Casey, Honeyford appeals to authority because only in authority can he find the certainties which enable him to cope with what he finds most disturbing about the modern world; the modern world being, by definition, a disturbing place, hence the perpetual stranglehold of reactionaries in all societies. The reactionary worships authority but always pretends that they are doing otherwise, that their appeal to authority is entirely disinterested. This is precisely the combination which lends itself to the nastier manifestations of extreme right-wing politics which, somewhere else, collaborated with fascism when it didn't embrace it, which didn't actually turn on the gas but did turn the other way so that it wouldn't be offended by the sight of suffering humanity. In the process, they forget that there would be no glorious tradition to speak of — indeed, there would be no language in which to write – if the makers of the tradition exalted in the same insularity.

And why, for that matter, are they always so selective about the authority to which they so loudly appeal? What about the radical, dissenting tradition that is also a part of the glory of English literature, of William Hazlitt: 'I hate a lie; a piece of injustice wounds me to the quick though nothing but the report of it reach me'; or Charles Dickens on Slavery: 'What! Shall we declaim against the ignorant peasantry of Ireland and mince the matter when these American taskmasters are in question? Shall we cry shame on the brutality of those who hamstring cattle: and spare the lights of Freedom upon earth who notch the ears of men and women. . . ?'

But literature is greater than its enemies; and the 'non-standard', 'West Indian' contribution that Honeyford derides doesn't stop at Linton Kwesi Johnson. What would he have against teaching Derek Walcott, one of whose sonnets in the *Midsummer* sequence might have been written with him in mind?:

Since all of your work was really an effort to appease
the past, a need to be admitted among your peers,
let the inheritors question the sibyl and the Sphinx,

and learn that a raceless critic is a primate's dream . . .

Perhaps Honeyford doesn't read 'foreign' writers, even when they write 'standard' English. It clearly isn't it a matter of some celebration to him that these 'foreigners' have fallen in love with the language and are using it to create poetry, and that this homage paid to the language is the life-blood of the tradition; that Shakespeare and Milton and Wordsworth will be kept alive and continue to be part of a living tradition by virtue of these 'West Indians' who have taken it for their own. Walcott again:

> . . . No language is neutral;
> the green oak of English is a murmurous cathedral
> where some took umbrage, some peace, but every
>   shade, all,
> helped widen its shadow . . .

What ought to be a matter of celebration to Honeyford becomes instead a problem and in the process he only reveals the paucity of his own enclosed universe by ossifying the same tradition he otherwise claims to celebrate.

They are small men, these little Englanders, small men without humanity or generosity or vision. This is ultimately why their ideas, or what passes for ideas, are so hollow. Ideas are worse than useless if they don't begin and end with the fact of human beings. That 'volatile Sikh' and those 'aggressive West Indians' are not theoretical abstractions to be argued over and conveniently labelled simply because they pose a threat to Sunday afternoons by the fireside and cream teas at the village cricket match. They are individual human beings, just like Honeyford; and, also like Honeyford, they are often confused, sometimes frightened, and always want the best for their children.

The failure to respect the simple fact of their humanity does indeed cause cities to burn, and not by hooligans either. If you are looking for 'violent thugs' they were not so very long ago tramping through Germany in the wake of the England football team. They are ugly, pathetic, terrifying, despicable . . . and British. They also talk the language of Wordsworth ('We must be free or die, who speak the tongue/ That Shakespeare spake; the faith and morals hold/ Which Milton held'); they too are the end result of Coleridge and Matthew Arnold; they are part of the glorious tradition, a tradition of which they aren't in the least bit worthy.

But the real question is, should we permit the thugs to dictate our responses? When they stand on the terraces on Wednesday evenings and Saturday afternoons and shout 'nigger' and 'wog' and 'jungle bunny' every time a black player takes possession of the ball I feel anger – and shame. I hope everybody else feels the same way too, but I know very well that they don't. I know because I once asked to go to a football match with some white friends one day and they all but panicked because they were torn between wanting to go but not wanting to cope with the obscenities they ignored every week but which my presence would force them to deal with.

This is how people are. They will nearly always overlook an unpleasantness rather than confront it. And they do so largely by telling themselves that it is not really their problem. During a recent television programme a well-meaning white celebrity was heard to ask a black MP what he thought about the race issue, as though it was his concern exclusively and not hers also. This is the kind of coyness which is itself part of the problem. Nothing is achieved when the majority believes it can pretend that the stink in all our nostrils is only the business of a few. It is hardly our reaction, after all, to child sex abuse, even when this directly affects only a minority of the country's children.

And the vexed minority, one should say, the word 'minority' being yet another misnomer, and shorthand for those people held to be outside the mainstream of British society: blacks, women, Jews, Catholics, Hindus, Moslems, homosexuals, the disabled, the elderly, the unemployed . . . The word is better defined by those not included, who turn out to be the mythical majority, which is clearly absurd. Unfortunately, the received wisdom concerning who counts and who doesn't, between those who flatter themselves that they're at the centre and those they imagine to inhabit the periphery, appears so self-evident that I once listened to a well-known poet publicly apologise for not being a black lesbian; for being, in fact, a white male heterosexual.

I'm not sure what we were supposed to do with this piece of information, though perhaps we were meant to clap in gratitude that he had descended to the level of the assembled minorities, victims all of us. Needless to say, the sheer arrogance of what he said completely escaped him, not least the idea that he belonged to the desirable majority to which we all aspired and for which we, denied entry by an unfortunate accident of birth, were to be pitied.

More disturbing still was the apparent approval, by the assembled minorities themselves, of what they had just heard; and it seemed that I was in the ultimate minority of disagreeing with everybody else – black or white, gay or straight, male or female. Still, the condition of the victim is a seductive one. It is better to be allocated your station in life than to have to forge it for yourself, especially if your station – 'black' writer, 'gay' writer, 'woman' writer – suddenly turns out to be a commercial asset. The fact that at any time it may just as suddenly cease to be a going concern, and then according to the whims of those who decide such things, needn't concern you while where is money to be made. When Caryl Phillips writes, in *The European Tribe*, 'I felt nothing . . . Nothing inside me stirred to make me rejoice,' I worry because I suspect that the thugs have triumphed; that others have been allowed to dictate the terms on which one is to live by permitting them the power to determine one's responses to the only country one has.

The abdication of one's birthright is not an option. You seize your birthright; you don't allow others to take it from you. Phillips says: I'm different because I'm black and therefore I don't belong here; Casey says: you're different because you're black and therefore you don't belong here. An unholy alliance is thereby established between the otherwise opposing camps, and neither the Oxford graduate nor the Cambridge don can say anything even remotely useful to that black family on the beach in Southend, a perfectly ordinary British family partaking of the waters in a perfectly ordinary English seaside town – theirs as much as anybody's.

And theirs because they determined it to be so as an act of conscious will. All the while one could see how nervous they were that one of Casey's more rough-and-ready compatriots might suddenly hurl an epithet in their direction – and not to be able to count on anybody's help. That day I came across the NF activists on the

High Street in Lewes I was so enraged that I snatched a bundle of their papers and tried to tear them up. Unfortunately, I had taken too many; I might as well have been trying to tear up a telephone directory. I suppose I was lucky that there just happened to be two policemen outside the law courts on the other side of the street. I could have been beaten senseless and my fellow townspeople, most of whom knew perfectly well who I was and where I lived and where my children went to school, would have simply walked past as though nothing had happened. In the end I crammed the papers into a litter bin nearby and stomped off, my rage no longer directed against the louts but against the people I lived amongst and who allowed these same louts to peddle their filth on the public street.

I understand Phillips's reaction. We have all been through it. A person would have to be extraordinarily thick-skinned to live in a country and be constantly told that they don't belong, that they aren't wanted, that they have nothing to offer, without reacting in this way. This is what threatened to happen to me when I first came over and worked in that factory in Wembley; this is what happens to all blacks who come to this country and try to make a contribution.

It's a pity and a shame that so many should have felt that they had only wasted a good part of their lives, like Winston's parents who returned to the West Indies even before I met their son; and it's a wonder that the riots of 1981 didn't happen sooner, or haven't erupted again, or were so contained at the time. One doesn't have to erect mystical racial theories to explain perfectly logical human behaviour; but the need to erect these theories, illogical, inhuman and contra-dictory as they are, is necessary if you are unable to see individual human beings for what they are: men and

women and children with ordinary needs and ordinary
desires.

3

O Babylon!

By the waters of Babylon we sat down and wept: when
   we remember thee, O Sion.
As for our harps, we hanged them up: upon the trees
   that are therein.
For they that led us away captive required of us then a
   song, and melody, in our heaviness: Sing us one of the
   songs of Sion.
How shall we sing the Lord's song: in a strange land?

Prayer Book 137:1

When I first thought of writing this book I was going to cast it entirely in the form of travel. I would undertake a journey to my grandfather's village of Acharacle in the Highlands, and make notes as I went along. But Britain proved a difficult country to write about if, as my initial approach dictated, I was to rely on the kind of casual encounter that can transform a place and invest it with life. This was nowhere more so than in the county town, as I had already discovered when I lived in Lewes and never achieved more than a nodding acquaintance with my neighbours. We would occasionally stop for a chat in the street or at the local supermarket or even outside the front door, but that was where it very firmly stopped.

I missed the ease of Nigeria where, in the course of another journey for another book, it was possible to turn up in a new place and be accosted by people who knew me for a stranger and who then made it their business to guarantee my welfare. This wasn't the case in Britain where the notion of individual space is firmly rooted in the national psyche. So I found myself driving from one place to another and becoming increasingly agitated by my blank notebook. I could go into pubs or cafés or public parks and stay as long as I pleased and by the end of the evening I would still be wondering how I was going to break through.

My temperament also worked against me. I'm the least gregarious of people. I find it difficult to fall into conversation with strangers, who themselves appear to be wary of me. No doubt their own reservations had a lot to do with the fact that I looked foreign, but the assumption of my foreignness might not have been enough in itself to deter them. A more outgoing person might have broken down the reserve.

The irony is that I wasn't foreign, and it would have been disastrous for me to write about Britain as if I were. The straightforward travel book which relies on the chance meeting with the succession of natives for its local colour – By Train Through India; Africa On Foot; Sailing Down The Amazon – is, precisely, the vision of a foreigner in a strange land. The very fact that a different vision was demanded helped me to clarify the nature of my relationship with my mother's country. Britain, for me, is not a foreign country, a relatively simple discovery which nevertheless took me a whole year – and many discarded pages – to arrive at.

In the meantime, I was burning petrol I couldn't afford and growing more and more despondent that I wasn't meeting people and having adventures which I could then write up when it was all over. In the end I simply gave way to the temptation of all travellers, which is to fall into movement for its own sake. Every traveller is a sensationalist by nature. They travel to combat the boredom of being stuck in one place and the fear that somehow their life is passing them by, that if they don't change the scenery every now and then their lives will have been wasted. So they take down the atlas and dream of other places and other people as a means of escape; but they quickly discover, when they arrive at their new destination, that change in itself has solved nothing. They've merely switched one currency for another, one landscape for another; but these are only superficial distractions and quickly satisfied.

But momentum, at least in the beginning, gave the illusion of purpose: Southend, Great Yarmouth, Cambridge, Norwich; all in the course of a single day, stopping only to grab something to eat in a Little Chef and then off again to the next town. And every place was like the last: every place had the same shopping arcades with the same shops; the same W. H. Smith's selling the same paperbacks: the same cinemas showing the same films. The sheer uniformity of Britain created its own problems, and all the while I was confronted with the challenge which faces anyone trying to write about their own country. How could I see with fresh eyes? How could I rid myself of the excess baggage of memory which continually weighed me down? What was I to say of London, for instance, which didn't immediately stir up memories of my childhood and my grandparents and a certain house in Streatham where I had once been happy?

Conversely, I had no interest in describing the tourist sights, which in any case have been described in more detail and with far greater authority than I could ever hope to achieve. Britain must be one of the most written-about countries in the world, as a glance at the topography section in any public library will confirm: *A Tour Through The Whole Island of Great Britain*; *A Journey to the Western Islands of Scotland*; *Rural Rides*; *Wild Wales; English Journey*. Some of the best writing in the language is contained in these narratives.

The problem of saying anything fresh struck me most forcibly in Lichfield, at the end of my first week, as I wandered about the Cathedral grounds with a party of German tourists while our guide gave us a run-down of its history and significant features. Lichfield was a fine cathedral. I loved its solidity and its majesty; I was awed by the faith which constructed it; my imagination responded to the idea of all those craftsmen mingling in an English midlands town of the middle-ages for this one purpose. But these were private thoughts which said nothing about the particular cathedral, and which in any case could equally be said for any other cathedral: Durham, Salisbury, St David's.

But it was in Lichfield that I became aware for the first time of the way in which the cathedral and Dr Johnson's house and the cobbled streets gave the sense of history which is so much a part of the British make-up, the British being a people with a powerful sense of their past and the institutions which are the product of time. These monuments to the past existed side-by-side with the supermarkets and the new housing estates and prevented the seduction of history from degenerating into a wistful nostalgia that can become a substitute for living in the modern world. An imbalance between the old and the new is unfortunate for any society: the one leads to inaction; the other breeds a certain kind of fanaticism. The British have avoided either extreme. The result is most clearly seen in towns like Lichfield (or Lewes or Canterbury or York), which is perhaps why the cities are not entirely representative of ordinary, everyday life in Britain; which is why my grandmother, who was so deeply of her country, took me as often as she could to visit these towns. As a child I was only really interested in the tea and the cakes at the end of the journey, but perhaps my grandmother knew what she was doing after all. My own sense of Britishness is built on these outings; a sense of belonging is inseparable from our memories of childhood, the warmth and nostalgia of a time when we were innocent.

From Lichfield I drove to Birmingham, where I

determined to stay a few days and reassess what I thought I was doing. I knew Birmingham. I had lived there for eighteen months after we left Ireland. At the time it was only meant as a staging post because friends had promised to put us up, but without money it was difficult to escape. Poverty is a trap; the poor may as well be in prison for all the difference it makes to their freedom of movement, which is why those politicians who tell the unemployed to move elsewhere for work sound so callous. But they aren't callous, only unimaginative, which would seem to be the prerequisite for a successful career in politics.

In fact it was while we were in Birmingham that a Tory MP went on the dole for a week to find out what poverty did to the human spirit. I noticed that he didn't have children to clothe or a sick parent to look after; in any case, one week was hardly long enough for his shoes to wear out or his television to go on the blink, or for his bad diet to undermine his health. Most of all, he wasn't poor for long enough to know what boredom means. There is no boredom like the boredom of poverty, which reduces the world to your four walls and the short trip to the shops to stare at the expensive goodies you can't afford. It was just an adventure to him, an exercise in public relations, and an insult to those with whom he was purporting to identify.

In common with many others, including those who lived there, we disliked Birmingham, its ugly nineteenth-century red-brick buildings that seemed to go on for ever, the harshness and vulgarity of the city centre, the feeling that one was encircled by motorways leading to more desirable places. Going back again it was easy to get lost on these motorways, and in my anxiety to get to my friends' place as quickly as possible I took the wrong exit. Three times I headed for the city centre, within sight of the Bull Ring, before I successfully negotiated my way across the complicated roundabout, but this probably had less to do with Birmingham than my own reluctance to return.

The following day I walked over to Balsall Heath, which was where we had rented a place from the housing association when we finally realised that it wouldn't be easy to leave the city, and that we couldn't go on imposing on our friends indefinitely. On the way I called on the writer Jim Crace, whose collection of stories, *Continents*, had just won several prizes. He was not himself a native of the city but had lived there many years and said how much he liked it after I sounded off my objections to the place in his back garden. He said that Birmingham had more trees relative to its size than any other British city, which I suppose was some kind of recommendation.

He also pointed out that the notion of Birmingham as a cultural desert was entirely mischievous: Benjamin Zepheniah, the British-Caribbean dub poet, and David Lodge, the academic novelist, were his near-neighbours. I understood him to mean by this that the cultural mix of the city invested it with an undeniable vibrancy, the result of the friction posed by the challenge of contrasting cultural perceptions, beginning with the way you walk, dress and eat, and ending with the way you assess your time-honoured institutions. From the writer's point of view, this could only be a good thing. And as in literature, so in the wider community: modern Britain was fortunate in having this channel to the energies and the talents – the creativity – of a pluralistic world. The immigrant communities in this country – Asian, Caribbean, European – came bearing gifts. The challenge lies with the host community to accept these gifts for what they were.

It was such a beautiful day and so peaceful in Jim's garden that it was enough to sit there with the sun on my face and a slight breeze rustling the leaves overhead; and then it occurred to me, as we made lazy conversation, that perhaps my previous reaction to the city wasn't only that I felt myself to be trapped and would have disliked it on that score alone, but that at the time I had been suffering from a species of culture shock which I hadn't been able to recognise as such because it lacked the drama one usually associates with the problem. When I first lived in Birmingham I had come directly from Ireland; the move was not between different languages and different religions, but between radically different ways of living within what was effectively the same, recognisably European culture. In many ways Birmingham had more in common with Dublin than either had with Ballydehob, our local village, but we rarely take into account the more complex, lateral connections between places which are obscured by our notions of cultures as national entities.

As with cultures, so with people: I have had conversations with friends in Lagos and London – on literature or politics or the war in the Gulf, say – that would not have been possible with our farmer in Ireland or his counterpart in Nigeria. Conversely, both farmers would have had plenty to talk about with each other once they had overcome their initial apprehension of difference. In the casualty department of a Birmingham hospital I once saw an Arab woman of traditional demeanour soothe a young British woman on her way to the delivery ward. Culture didn't come into their relationship at that moment; it was enough that they were both women, though neither spoke the other's language or understood the other's gods.

Ballydehob to Birmingham: the contrast between

rural Ireland and urban Britain couldn't have been starker. Where we previously had to walk four miles for a newspaper we were now within easy reach of all the amenities we could desire; and yet, despite the fact that, though still relatively poor, we were materially more comfortable, it was difficult not to feel that our lives were somehow out of our control.

No doubt this feeling of helplessness had something to do with the sheer size of the city and our own obscurity within it; but it also had to do with the fact that we were signing on and therefore dependent on the State for our food and our rent, both of which are calculated to make anybody feel helpless. But one also began to see Britain, in contrast to Ireland, as a tightly structured society in which any deviation from the norm was made difficult by the way in which the society functioned. With the minimum of effort we were given enough money (just) to provide for our needs. Nothing else was required of us but to behave ourselves while the real people, the people in work, got on with the job of making things run smoothly.

My grandparents exemplified this absolute regularity of British life, the highly settled social arrangement in which the eccentric functions as a counter: the elderly woman who goes for a morning dip in mid-winter, or the man who lives alone in a caravan in the woods near Croydon. Every other Saturday my grandfather took me to watch Chelsea; every Sunday afternoon I was packed off to the common to play with the other boys; I always knew what day of the week it was by the meal my grandmother placed before us: a fry-up on Saturday; lamb and mint sauce on Sunday; left-overs on Monday.

And yet, despite this, I later discovered that my grandfather's life was not as predictable as it appeared.

As a young man of eighteen he left his village of Acharacle in the Highlands and walked the thirty-five miles to Glasgow. This was just before the Great War. After serving in the trenches in France he joined the Post Office and worked as a postman in the Lake District. At the outbreak of the Second World War he moved to London when every other person was trying to leave. It seemed fitting, when I first thought of writing this essay, that I should make a pilgrimage to my ancestral village.

After I left Jim's place I walked over to my old street and stood outside the house we had rented only five years before. There was a box-room overlooking the street and I remembered the hours I had spent staring out of the window instead of working because I was at the beginning of a four-year crisis in which I wrote very little. If I had known then that the crisis would go on for so long I might have given up, but you can't know these things in advance. As in most periods of darkness you muddle through. It's only later that you look back and wonder.

Staring out of that window I saw some revealing sights. Balsall Heath was genuine inner-city slum. Most of the residents then and now were first-generation Bengali immigrants. One could still see the peasant in them by the way the women squatted in the tiny front patch that passed for a garden as they dug the barren soil and coaxed a few miserable plants to flower. The women, that is, who were permitted outdoors. The milkman still did his rounds with a huge bunch of keys so that he could put the bottles inside the houses. The women from the more traditional – or more reactionary – households weren't even allowed to appear on the doorstep. On the occasions when they were allowed out, usually to attend the nearby mosque or, more rarely, to visit a friend nearby (but always under cover of night), they were invariably dressed in full purdah, complete with a black veil covering their faces. Other than that they remained secluded indoors. They had travelled thousands of miles, they had removed themselves – or been removed – from one culture to another, and all they saw, day after day, were the four walls of a terrace house in the middle of Britian's second largest city.

In violent juxtaposition, the hookers plied their trade on the street corner, but it was the temporary brothel down the road which was really bizarre. The house itself had already been bought by the housing association for conversion into flats and there was some delay before work started. In the interval a middle-aged Irishman with salt-and-pepper hair took advantage and set up shop. He imported for that purpose a thin, washed-out woman in her late thirties who sat all day on a hardback chair in an otherwise bare living room. She smiled at every likely-looking man who walked past, and to generate the required atmosphere an unshaded red light bulb dangled from the ceiling above her head. The only person I ever saw enter was a Sikh schoolboy who rode up on his bicycle one lunchtime and disappeared upstairs with her.

The street walkers did a better trade. They started gathering in the late afternoon and were still there at midnight. Their presence ensured, amongst other things, a steady stream of traffic as motorists cruised up and down, slowing whenever they drew alongside a single woman, no matter how young. I once saw a driver try and accost a schoolgirl in uniform. She couldn't have been more than twelve years old.

All this was particularly distressing for the Bengali

families. One day I watched as two prostitutes raised their skimpy skirts above their waists for the benefit of one such family out on a Sunday afternoon stroll, the wife in regulation purdah, the husband averting his eyes from the shocking sight as the children began the painful process of somehow uniting two worlds that would never meet. It was easy enough to understand the fear in the heart of that man, the determination to protect his daughters by pretending that the world outside his front door did not properly exist.

And to do this on inadequate resources: the father wanted to accomplish what only money might have made possible. It is hardly surprising, after all, that the Asian immigrants should be so hardworking, willing to keep their shops and factories open longer hours; or that there should reputedly be one hundred millionaires called Patel in the London phone directory. An immigrant community works harder the more it feels itself to be estranged from the host community. Money then becomes a substitute for security which can at least shield your children from the unpleasant realities of daily life which are alien to your inherited categories of human relations: the place of women; the duties of children; the responsibilities of husbands. These notions might be out of sympathy with contemporary British attitudes, we might consider them outdated and un-pleasant, but the tension in the heart of that man out on a stroll with his wife and daughters was no less poignant for all that.

It was through my older daughter that I learned about the British-Asian girl who was suddenly taken out of school on her fourteenth birthday, forbidden to go out, and told that she was engaged to a man from Bangladesh whom she had never met but who was at that very moment applying for permission to enter the country to join his fiancée. I pitied the women of her mother's generation and I loathed their subjugation (I could never look at a woman in full purdah with anything other than pity and outrage, no matter how many of these woman themselves argued in favour of their condition), but I didn't see what one could reasonably do about it. Their daughters were another matter. I was concerned that they should be left free to find a place within this society, to become British, which is what they were. The worst that could happen to these children was to be forced by their parents to collude in the lie that they didn't actually live in Britain but in an outpost of Asia on British soil, and therefore follow customs which had little to do with their present lives. The irony in the case of these children was that their own integration was being resisted not only by the *Salisbury Review* but by their own parents.

I didn't trust the motives of the parents. I knew very well that whatever their rationale for what they did they had retreated into an extreme conservatism as their only way of coping with the fear generated in them by the daily assault on their most deeply held beliefs. This fear was transferred wholesale to their children, who then had to cope most directly with the demands of the two opposing cultures. One often saw the results of this silent war on the faces of these children, usually at the point where the two worlds most violently collided. It wasn't so much the father who was protecting his daughters from the sight of the prostitutes on the street but the other way round: it was the daughters who were pained by their father's pain, by the knowledge that a certain aspect of Britain, represented at that moment by the hookers in the street, was more intimidating to the father than it could be to either of them. And it would get worse as they grew older, as they began to understand more clearly their parents' vulnerability. The discovery that your parents are human beings just like you, that they're weak and ignorant and often frightened by what they don't understand, is difficult enough to handle without these other complications. This was a recipe for tragedy, and so it happened.

Not so long ago I read a newspaper report about an eighteen-year-old boy from a Muslim-Asian household who stabbed his father with a kitchen knife when his father tried to prevent him from going to the local disco. As far as the father was concerned his son's friends were decadent Westerners who would only lead him astray, and he certainly didn't want his son depraved by wanton white girls. The newspaper article concerned the boy's trial. A psychiatrist called upon to submit evidence gave his problem a fancy name – cross-cultural neurosis, I think he called it – but the clinical detachment of such a prognosis was misleading, not least because it implied a possible cure. The boy's tragedy admitted no cure. It was a curse.

More tragic, certainly, than the children of West Indian immigrants, for whom the issue is more straightforward – or, at least, less complex. For the British-Caribbean, whose first language is English and whose God is Christian, it is *only* a matter of colour; and how complex an issue this finally proves to be is entirely in the hands of those who have decided to make it an issue. The problem doesn't lie with the British-Caribbeans, who are forced to live with the consequences. For this reason their rage and frustration erupted so easily. The flames of Brixton and Toxteth were proof positive that Babylon was indeed burning; and from their point of view (if from nobody else's) it is far better that Babylon burn and consume us all than that they should continue to live in the hell of other people's making.

The Moslem-Asian immigrants, more recent still than the West Indians and lacking any real point of cultural contact with the host community, are in a much more difficult and delicate position. As I stood outside my old house that day I only had to observe the way in which the women clutched their children as they hurried to the safety of their homes. It was late afternoon and time for the hookers to gather on the corner, but when I walked to the end of the street I was surprised that there weren't any in sight.

From the *Evening Mail* (9 September 1987):

BRUM'S IMAGE BOOSTERS: BID TO SHOW BALSALL HEATH IS BEAUTIFUL

'Balsall Heath is beautiful' – and residents have launched a campaign to prove it and clear the area's poor name with outsiders.

The initiative is designed to show the brighter sides of Balsall Heath which is often associated with the decline of Birmingham.

Dr Dick Anderson, who is the director of the St Paul's Association in Balsall Heath, said the poor opinion of the area has distressed the residents . . .

He also said the image of Balsall Heath as a red-light area with prostitutes parading on many street corners was false.

The local community newspaper, the *Heathen*, conducted a survey three years ago and spotted 50 prostitutes on the Balsall Heath and North Moseley streets.

Editor Mr John Ure went on tour again recently and did not see one . . .

Miss Moyra Connolly, who lives in Trafalgar

Road, said: 'I think the campaign has got a lot of support from the local people.

'I agree that the whole place is more beautiful than presented in the media . . .

'We hope it will get a better name because we want to attract people who want to invest money in the area.'

Church life has helped to improve the feeling in the community, particularly around the Central Mosque.

In fact the hookers had only moved down the road to Edgbaston, but I was more intrigued by the reference to the mosque in the article. It's easy enough to see an immigrant community largely in terms of their status as victims. I saw their vulnerability as they daily negotiated a society they didn't properly understand in a language they couldn't properly speak, but I forgot that I perceived them only from the outside. Their personal lives, after all, are not so restricted that they are unable to effect change in their own community by coming together for a specific aim. That father could now take a Sunday afternoon stroll around Balsall Heath with his wife and daughters and be spared at least one manifestation of British decadence, and it was his own doing.

For the few days I was in Birmingham I fell into a routine of sorts. In the mornings, after the friends I was staying with had gone to work, I sat at the breakfast table and made notes; in the afternoons I walked to Balsall Heath and simply wandered about the area. I wasn't looking for anything in particular. I just thought it might be good to be part of the crowd, but without consciously looking for material, without the need to impose order on what I saw. I tried to be zen about it, in other words. Every now and then I caught a glimpse of how the book might shape itself, but then it would evaporate the moment I tried to pin it down. So I kept walking until my feet ached and it was time to go home.

On the Sunday before I left I went to a service in one of the British-Caribbean evangelical churches. The Church of God of Prophecy was in Handsworth, on the other side of the city, and close to the scene of the 1981 riots. I remembered passing through there around the time of the riots and I remembered how stunned the people had looked, as if they were appalled by the violence but couldn't account for it, appalled perhaps by their own violence. Many of the Asian-owned shops were boarded up but it was trade as usual. I admire the sheer tenacity of human beings, their stubborn ability to keep going while the world is collapsing about them. Not that these shopkeepers had much choice, and this despite the unmistakable hostility between them and the British-Caribbean community: as much black rage was directed against the Asians as against Babylon.

There is little love lost between these two communities in Britain. The British-Asians, as a group, have never cared to be identified with the British-Caribbeans. Their recent objection to being described as 'black' in local council leaflets on the grounds that they aren't black but brown, for instance, may rest on the literal truth, but their objections have little to do with dictionary definitions. Bigotry is a human trait, which is why it is so easy to tap.

One oughtn't to be surprised at those endless rallies where the people are incited to rise up against the infidel, in whatever guise the infidel happens to present itself: African against Asian, white against black, Moslem against Christian. The difference – colour, race, religion – is only incidental. If none of these are present then human beings will find something else which will do just as well. In a certain country in central Africa the pygmies are being exterminated – the word is not too strong – for no other reason than that they're pygmies. No useful function is served by pretending that bigotry is exclusive to any one group of human beings.

The Church of God of Prophecy served an almost exclusively British-Caribbean population. The service was led by a stern, middle-aged woman who prompted the congregation of two hundred or more through six hymns without a break, by which time we were ready for the testimonies that followed. Four women and two men stood before us. One after the other they recalled for us the day they had been saved; they recounted their lives before their eyes had been opened and they were allowed to see; and they repeated how happy they were now that salvation had been granted them. They cautioned us not to allow ourselves to become complacent because the Devil was ever-watchful for lax souls, and they thanked God for helping them through another week and allowing them to be here tonight to praise His Holy Name. One of the women became possessed. She shouted so loudly her voice began to crack. The faithful were with her all the way. A big, elderly woman stood up and stretched out her arms and started to speak in tongues. The possessed woman moved slowly back to her seat, shouting all the while. One of the men stepped forward and began his testimony; he was so overcome he dabbed at his eyes with a handkerchief. The possessed woman, by now in her seat, started jerking her body violently.

It was the first time I had heard someone speak in

tongues, a strange phenomenon I had already been told about by the Catholic fathers at my boarding school in Lagos. The disciples spoke in tongues after they were visited by the Holy Ghost, but it was just one of those things that happened long ago. It didn't happen nowadays. We had motor cars and atom bombs and we sent rockets into space. We were wise. We knew that the scriptures were only taken literally by the simple-minded.

I couldn't deny the power in that building, and I wished I could have shared more fully in the collective experience. Religious faith is an expression of the collective. The woman who spoke in tongues was only a channel for the will of the congregation, the faith that miracles happened and that God spoke to His children. God was speaking directly through this woman but I couldn't hear what He said because I didn't know how to listen to her, just as once upon a time I couldn't see trees because I didn't know how to look at them. I was apart from it. I didn't belong. I merely observed something I didn't trust.

I was also bored. I have always found religious ceremony tedious, beginning with school where I had to attend mass every morning before breakfast and prayers every evening before supper. But if you were going to worship God I could see the point in the elaborate ritual. It was the Catholic ritual which appealed to Africans more than the spartan services of northern Protestantism, which is why Catholicism is a stronger force on the continent. Where the Protestant churches did take root they were rapidly Africanised.

Many people, and not only Roy Kerridge, have remarked on the West African style of much of Caribbean life, a tribute to the endurance of ancient civilisations which weren't destroyed by the horrors of the Middle Passage, or by the second journey from the plantations of Belize to the back streets of Birmingham. One wonders, in fact, that a people who have had their back twice-broken should still find the reserves to celebrate their own rebirth into life, just as one wonders that those who ought to possess a more coherent sense of their own identity should display such a wretched opinion of their civilisation as to foresee its imminent collapse by the new settlers, who themselves constitute less than one-twentieth of this country's population.

If civilisations survive their ability to adapt and change; and if a country like Nigeria, for example, has benefited from the presence of European civilisation on its soil and is now challenged to use that heritage to create something new, it would be fitting to think that the process worked the other way. The Church of England might bemoan falling attendances as a reflection of the dominant secularism of modern British society, but one doesn't have to look far to see that religion – like literature – is being given new life by the descendants of the colonised, and not only the West Indians. The outsider coming to Britain might be forgiven for thinking that the religious sense thrived only amongst the newcomers, the Moslems and the Sikhs and the Hindus no less than the fundamental Christians; but it would be an accurate observation nonetheless.

This new religious input ought to be a cause for celebration on the part of true Englishmen, and not merely because it might have consequences for the society which are more far-reaching than one could possibly see – open thine eyes! – from the perspective of an ivory tower. Any force which counters the tendency of human beings to turn in on themselves when they are challenged must for that reason be beneficial.

When Ray Honeyford questions the notion of multi-cultural education and scores political points by playing on ignorant prejudice, he doesn't imagine a history course which included the West Indies as part of its syllabus, or religious instruction which introduced children to Indian forms of worship; and to see these approaches as good things in themselves if only because they suggest the variety and the beauty of the world – of our world. This is not multi-cultural education, another misnomer, but education in the proper sense, like learning about the tropical rain forest as part of a balanced geography syllabus.

No society is self-sufficient; every society can teach us. The bonus is that those descendants of the immigrants who are encouraged to share their special heritage with the rest of the community will in turn feel more secure in our country. This doesn't mean that they will thereby destroy our traditions, though it does mean that they will undermine partial interpretations of Burke and Coleridge and William Morris. They might even suggst interpretations we hadn't previously suspected. In any case, the challenge is already here, and it isn't solved by repatriation (voluntary or otherwise), however many authorities are misquoted to that end.

Honeyford is like the Regius Professor of Modern History at Cambridge who recently delivered a public lecture in which he said, amongst other things: 'What we need is more English history, not this non-existent history of ethnic entities and women'. The little Englander all over again who still thinks that the world is flat. But why, come to that, are these reactionaries so tiresomely chauvinistic? Is their sense of safety so fragile that they must lash out at the first sign of any real challenge to their hallowed orthodoxies? . . . 'ethnic entities and women', he declares, forgetting that he is referring to the real, literal, actual majority and not some fanciful numbers game that is somehow sanctioned by the use of the inclusive 'we'. Which 'we', precisely, is he talking about, and on whose say-so?

When the service was over I asked the evangelist if I could talk to her. Away from the pulpit she was a mild-mannered, unassuming woman, even a little nervous. This surprised me, but it shouldn't have: her authority in the pulpit derived from her faith; it was a measure of her faith that she transcended her immediate circumstances, that of a perfectly ordinary wife and mother. She lived nearby and she invited me over to her house; but it was only later, when I took out my notebook, that I realised she had thought of me as a possible convert. I tried to explain that I was writing a book. She seemed sceptical but offered me tea all the same.

After an awkward silence I decided it was best to be direct. I asked her how she felt about speaking in front of all those people. She said that it was always a great ordeal for her, but then all she had to do was pray to God and He would help her through: 'If you ask God for His assistance He will always give it to you.' Sometimes, she said, she felt depressed and anxious, but then she would go down on her knees and she would feel 'the hand of God lifting me up, up, up . . . but you must realise your need of God before He can help you.'

I asked her what she thought about the established churches. She said, 'they have a form of Godliness but they deny the power of the Holy Ghost.' This was because, she said, they no longer laid emphasis on the individual having direct experience of the Holy Ghost, which is the only way you can be cleansed of sin. Once you've had that experience you're changed for ever. A person so possessed has great power. She had been touched by such a person, 'and a fire came out of his hand and knocked me right out'.

I asked her about the congregation. I had been struck by the sight of all those smartly dressed youths in her church, and I wondered how it was that their parents had managed to keep them away from the attractions of the street. One sees any number of disaffected British-Caribbeans on any number of streets. That was easy to explain, just as it was easy to see why their parents had given up. I mentioned the group we had passed outside the café on the way to her house. Her face conveyed pain and bewilderment. She said that she was saddened by the sight of so many unemployed black youths in her area who were living without knowledge of God: 'If only they would come to the Lord, how happy they would be, each day would be a brand new day for them.'

I asked her about white membership. The only white person I saw at the service was the wife of a black man. She said that a white man had turned up at a few services once upon a time but had since drifted elsewhere: 'He was searching for something, I think he was lonely,' she said. He still phoned her now and then and occasionally visited her so that they could pray together.

And then she said, quite spontaneously, 'I don't really understand the way white people worship,' and she immediately looked apologetic, as if she had said too much. Misunderstanding occurs on both sides, but if Roy Kerridge possessed even a fraction of this woman's humility he wouldn't have been able to write the nonsense he did in his silly article for the *Salisbury Review*, with his irresponsible talk of 'pagan practices', 'tribal gods' and 'fetish devotees'. All it takes is a little humility and a genuine willingness to learn from each other.

'I don't really understand the way white people worship,' she said, and her words echoed those of the Nigerian writer, Buchi Emecheta, who was similarly perplexed by the services she encountered in 'white' churches when she first came to London:

In England . . . 'church' was a big, grey building with stained-glass windows, high ornamental ceilings, very cold, full of rows and rows of empty chairs . . .
She could not then go to any of them because it made her cry to see such beautiful places of worship empty when, in Nigeria, you could hardly get a seat if you came in late. But you were happy through it all, you were encouraged to bellow out the songs – that bellowing took away some of your sorrows.

Such unanimity of experience – but the evangelist had never set foot in Africa. She had grown up speaking English in a British colony and now she lived in Britain, and yet her idea of religious worship was not only alien to that of the British but resonated with that of a Nigerian coming to this country for the first time. This is part of the style of Caribbean life which strikes a familiar note to the West African.

C. G. Jung, the Swiss psychoanalyst, elaborated a theory, long familiar to my father's people, of the existence deep within us all of the collective memory of the race which we inherit from our forebears and pass on in turn to the future generations, as if biology itself possessed more than just the codes for this colour of eyes, this shape of nose, this set of teeth, to embrace the ancestors themselves. It's a difficult idea for a secular society to cope with, which is why Jung is sometimes dismissed as a crank, and why Yoruba belief is labelled traditional and turned into an academic discipline.

To be secular is to be modern: the language assumes as much. And yet modern Englishmen, the products of a secular society, tattoo their shaven heads with the image of the Union Jack and put the boot in while they chant of England. At the other end, Elgar's 'Pomp and Circumstance', played on the last night of the proms, generates the kind of emotion in the hearts of the listeners which obviously transcends the immediate piece of music to embrace something much larger, something to do with an elusive but powerful sense of one's own Englishness and what that means in terms of belonging. The notion of the collective unconscious, after all, suggests the unity of those who partake of the racial memory at the same time as it defines the 'other'. The 'other' is everybody else, as the football hooligan instinctively knows.

To what extent do the ancestors figure in the racial unconscious of those British children born of Caribbean or Asian parents, and how does that alter the fact of their Britishness? This is at the heart of any debate on what it means to belong to a culture. In his article for the *Salisbury Review*, John Casey attempts to provide a definition which moves uneasily between sentiment and chronology but finally collapses on itself because he allows the fact of colour to obscure the central question. In practice the most dramatic example is posed not by the British-Caribbeans (black) but by the British-Asians (brown), although in terms of the skin trade, the gradations of colour as a measure of one's worth, it ought to work in the opposite direction.

And most dramatic as it translated itself in terms of

language, assuming language to be an analogue for a culture and therefore containing the subtle codes of the particular culture which is thereby being transmitted. I remember one day watching a British-Asian boy with his grandmother at a social security office in London a few years ago. The old woman didn't speak English so the boy was required to act as translator. As he switched between two languages he performed a complex series of subtle personality shifts. Either language demanded a set of allegiances which conflicted with the other.

This was the real front line, this ten-year-old child in a DHSS office attempting to squeeze a few pounds from the state for an elderly peasant woman who found herself stranded in a strange landscape. The front line is not a romantic place to be; it isn't drugs and music and the promise of danger, but a generation of children at the frontier, pioneers without the benefit of the cartographer's labour. It isn't possible to survive in such a landscape for long, however much the forces of both cultures conspire to keep them there. It's enough to make a boy stick a knife in his father's guts, and so it happened. And in choosing to go to the disco with his mates, in opting to chase wanton white women, that boy broke not only with his father but, assuming Jung to be right, with his ancestors as well.

Cultural diversity is good when it is affirmed by the majority; cultural division is harmful when it devolves on the individual. This is why the half-caste-mixed-race-neither-white-nor-black-sterile-hybrid-mulatto   is such a potent symbol of the psychic division which they themselves represent in their person. The dominant culture senses this instinctively, whereupon articulate voices within it begin with repatriation and end with genocide.

And yet, in reality, the majority has nothing to fear.

Those whom they identify as different, and who carry within them the remnants of difference, are themselves driven towards assimilation. The fact that this process is wholly unconscious doesn't make it any less powerful. Those Moslem-Asian parents currently agitating for private Islamic schools are attempting to arrest what they rightly perceive as the eventual extinction of their culture on these shores. This siege mentality is no more than we should expect, and the tragedy contained in such a fate is not helped by those who can only address the problem with violence. Courage and vision are needed on both sides, but these are notoriously rare commodities in any society.

I felt considerably calmer by the time I left Birmingham. I had resolved, for one thing, that it was not necessary for me to go everywhere and see everything. I wasn't writing that kind of book. I needed simply to trust in my creative imagination; I needed the same kind of faith with which the evangelist at the Church of God approached the pulpit every Sunday evening and was filled with the power of the Holy Ghost.

I had been given an address in Hull. I drove first towards Spalding, in Lincolnshire, and then followed the coast road north. This time I just kept going because it was pleasant to drive on such a glorious day. I took the weather to be a good omen. Perhaps writers are superstitious by nature. As long as the weather held, as it did over the next fortnight, I was optimistic about the journey. The rains only started on the very day that I left Acharacle, my grandfather's village, when my pilgrimage was done and the journey over.

I finally stopped in Grimsby just as dusk was falling. The days were getting noticeably shorter now as we approached the autumnal equinox. I found a lively looking pub in the town centre and bought a drink before I saw the local yobs in the corner. One of them had a tattoo on the side of his shaved head; all of them wore aggressive T-shirts and polished black boots. I wondered that I hadn't seen them earlier. I took it so much for granted that I could instantly suss bad news in any gathering because it was necessary to be able to do so, but in the event they didn't even notice me, and afterwards I thought: how foolish. One sees danger everywhere, but perhaps this time I was guilty of just that stereotyping which breeds the kind of politics I find objectionable.

I slept in the car overnight and set off at first light, just as the sun was rising on the horizon, but I hadn't gone two hundred yards when I was flagged down by a police car. I told them I was a writer and that I was travelling around the country in order to write a book, but it sounded rather feeble even to me. A travelling salesman or a journalist would have sounded better, more robust somehow. They looked bemused, but I spoke well and I had a typewriter in the boot and when they called up the computer to check on the car registration number they smiled and called me 'sir'.

As I entered Hull I was surprised to find myself driving down Free Town Way until I saw a sign which said that the city was twinned with the capital of Sierra Leone. I wondered what this meant in practical terms. The cost alone would have made regular exchanges between the cities prohibitively expensive. My first thought was to dismiss it as a stunt by a group of deluded left-wing councillors, but if so it was also a rather endearing example of British eccentricity. The councillors wanted to express their feeling about Empire and poverty and the Third World, and they came up with a bizarre but touching solution.

It happened that Barbara, the person I was staying with, was also involved in some way with the city council. I had already noticed a stack of the current issue of *Socialist Worker* in her living room, and it was perhaps unwise of me to mention my thoughts on the Sierra Leone connection. One thing led to another – the problems at the Dewsbury primary school were at their height just then – and we ended up having an argument about the provision of separate Islamic schools in Britain. It turned out that she subscribed to the idea that all cultural values were relative, and that we therefore had no right to judge other cultures by 'our' standards. I pointed out that if she really believed this then she would eventually be forced to defend the arranged marriage of a fourteen-year-old British girl; she countered by saying that it was no business of ours either way, and that to criticise what they did was to lend tacit support to the views of the Right.

I mention this because Barbara's reasoning seemed to me a fairly typical instance of the stultifying polarisation of modern British politics. In Britain your political allegiance dictates your conscience, not the other way round. You vote Tory or Labour and then decide whether you believe in comprehensive education or nationalised industries. That there isn't sufficient support for a middle ground in British parliamentary politics is proved by the failure of the Social Democrats to establish a credible alternative to the other two. This in turn accounts for the growing importance of extra-parliamentary pressure groups – Greenpeace, Animal Rights, CND – to focus the unease of the small but vocal minority of British people whose politics are very much dictated by their conscience.

This polarisation is best reflected in the journals which cater for either side of the political divide, and it explains why, for instance, it is possible for a left-wing magazine such as the *New Statesman and Society* to carry a scathing article on the advertising industry in an issue which also contains a glossy insert for frivolous goodies: spelling computers; credit card wallets; personalised stationary in three colours.

The function of the *New Statesman* (or any left-wing British magazine, for that matter: *Marxism Today* will do just as well) is to make it OK for you to buy expensive incidentals for your loved ones at Christmas at the same time as you manage to hold political views which claim to dislike the rampant consumerism which has resulted in a balance of payments deficit and high interest rates.

As regards Barbara, the fact that the law of the country had been broken and that a British girl was being denied an education *because* she was a girl was conveniently overlooked. And yet she herself enjoyed the privileges of a society which had outlawed sexual discrimination: she had gone to university; she had a responsible job; she exercised her right to stay single. How was it possible? She would hardly argue that apartheid was a Boer tradition and then proceed to defend it. On the contrary, Free Town Way was itself an implicit condemnation of the sort she was willing to make in the specific case where she, as a British citizen, was directly involved.

But I don't believe that Barbara was convinced of her own argument. She was just confused. And at the bottom of her confusion was a kind of arrogance which she never properly examined. She assumed, as a matter of course, the fragility of a culture which wasn't white and European and which for those reasons ought to be handled with caution, as if the products of that culture had come off the plane from Uganda or Pakistan or Bangladesh with a warning in three languages. These poor, misunderstood Third World people weren't like us. They were brown and foreign and just because they locked up little girls didn't give us the right to pass judgment on them.

To impose our beliefs would be to open ourselves to the charge of racism, the word 'racism' itself having been invested with a potent magic which suddenly deprives its hearers of the ability to think, not dissimilar to the stories I heard as a child in Nigeria of apparently healthy men expiring on the spot at the sound of an enemy's curse. In both cases we are dealing with the power of the world to alter reality, to change what we see in front of our eyes.

So the crooked director of the 'black' project, attempting to bully his detractors into silence, calls the white councillors querying his tax returns 'a bunch of racists' while he completes his villa in Barbados. In the meantime, the pensioners in his charge, the men and women who fought for this country in the last war (8,000 West Indian troops in 1943), and who worked for this country in peacetime (mostly by taking jobs nobody else wanted), are denied the cooked meal which might make all the difference in the coming winter.

But perhaps I've been unfair to Barbara. When I mentioned the example of my daughter's friend I could see that she was more troubled than she was willing to admit. I could also see that she was sufficiently distressed by the sophistry of the *Salisbury Review* to want to distance herself as much as possible from their views. And her distress was rooted in another, more personal conflict. She said, 'When I was a child my mother encouraged my elder sister and me to stand on the street corner after school and count the number of blacks we saw before tea-time.' The last time she visited her sister in Winchester she made the mistake of taking a British-Caribbean friend along with her and was appalled by the reception they received. Her sister had even cancelled a dinner party because she couldn't cope with what her friends might say. That was four years ago. She hasn't spoken to her sister since.

As Barbara told me all this I began to understand the ways in which my own circumstances actually operated in my favour. I was at least spared this level of ambiguity in my close relationships. Any relationships I had were necessarily predicated on a view of the world which dispensed with this sort of nonsense. But I also understood the ways in which Barbara was a provincial. Her provincialism had nothing to do with Hull; she might equally have lived in London for all the difference it would have made. I mean that she hadn't grasped the imperatives of the modern world because her experience of the world was bounded by local concerns. These imperatives make demands on us which transcend national boundaries. I don't care for the treatment of Moslem women (nor do many Moslem women), and I'm at liberty to say so because the degradation of human beings anywhere is a moral and not a cultural issue.

But if I could say this without qualification it was because I had been given the confidence to do so by my unique experience. I belonged in two cultures at the same time as I stood in uneasy relationship with either. The tension this generated gave me insights which might have been more difficult to achieve with Barbara's more restricted experience. It wasn't arrogance that I thought I saw in her; it was lack of confidence. However, it seems that the need for a less fractured sense of belonging forces many to reject the ambiguous position that comes with the dual heritage. In Newcastle, where I went after Hull, I met up again with a man I had known many years before at university.

Arvind was from Kenya but of Indian descent. As a student he was a well-known 'radical' and political activist. Then it happened that in the space of a single week, during his final year, his father and his elder brother died. He returned home to look after his mother and his sister and his sister-in-law and his nephews and nieces, and to run the lucrative family business upon which they all depended and which had enabled him to spend three years in Europe indulging in play. Now he was married with two young children of his own.

The last time I saw him, a few months after the double tragedy when he returned to wind up his affairs, he told me that he was about to go to India at his mother's insistence in order to meet his prospective bride. He had said, looking straight at me, 'I don't believe in mixed marriages,' which was merely his way of declaring that the time for play was now over. He underestimated me. I had a good idea what his new life entailed, and I could understand that he wanted to avoid a fruitless discussion, even if I thought he was mistaken in trying to deny an important facet of his experience. His time at university was not less real or less valuable simply because it was now so far removed from his present circumstances, but I also recognised his hysteria.

Now he spoke about smuggling gold-dust into Canada in talcum powder containers, and I thought I heard part of the small-talk in certain Nairobi bars at a particular time of day. His second child was born in Toronto for immigration purposes, and I wondered, when he said this, where it would all end. India, Kenya, Britain, Canada: there are a limited number of countries in the world, after all, but I was immediately put in mind of my grandfather leaving his village for whatever obscure reasons and bequeathing his descendants something of his own restlessness.

Perhaps, one day, Arvind's son or grandson or great-grandson will make the journey back to the ancestral homeland and re-establish the continuity which was severed at the source, but the thing had to first exhaust itself. It was like a virus in the blood stream for which there was no medicine: it either killed you or you sweated it out.

The sense of place is as fundamental in some ways as the need for bread to eat and water to drink. We cannot properly be said to live without it. When we are denied it we become neurotic, even suicidal. Arvind's sudden discovery of tradition (witness his marriage) was a neurotic response to the absence of the sense of place. He wanted to obliterate the various strands of his complex condition which didn't fit the narrow demands of his present circumstance. In doing so he was forced to deny his wholeness.

But it was better than killing himself. Sam, the man who shot himself in Ireland, was also faced with the same challenge. Perhaps the difference between them was that Sam had fewer responsibilities and more time. It's possible that the sudden deaths of Arvind's father and elder brother were actually his salvation. He might instead have continued the life he was leading as a student until he turned forty, which was Sam's age when he borrowed a gun from the neighbouring farmer and blew his brains out. Arvind would then have returned to Nairobi as Sam had returned to London, and he would have felt his failure to measure up just as acutely.

And yet, ironically enough, Arvind's discovery of tradition, his need to look backwards in time as a refuge from the demands of the always-threatening present, is exactly matched by those who might otherwise be thought to possess that sense of belonging he

conspicuously lacked. It seems that even white Englishmen born and raised in this country of 'pure' English
blood suddenly turn out to require the same ballast.
Why else does John Casey, in 'One Nation: The Politics
of Race', begin by calling on the ancestors to justify his
position? Why also does Ray Honeyford, in 'Education
and Race – An Alternative View', feel himself
threatened at the use of an English which isn't sanctioned by History? Why else is the *Salisbury Review*
named after a nineteenth-century Prime Minister
except to suggest the idea of tradition, as if that alone
invested it with the moral authority, the stamp of
authentic Englishness, with which it then proceeds to
define degrees of belonging?

Arvind's condition is extreme, but it is not peculiar to
those whose fractured sense of place is so obvious. The
great movement of peoples in our century, and with it
the break-up of discrete cultures, is a condition which
we all share, if only by proxy. The forces that gave rise to
this movement, the forces which set my grandfather on
the road to Fort William at the same time as his
counterpart in an Indian village caught the boat to
Nairobi, are the forces which have shaped the modern
consciousness. Those who don't participate in it directly,
such as my cousin in Acharacle with whom I was
proposing to stay, nevertheless live in a world which is
grappling with the fall-out from this upheaval. And
even my cousin, who is as rooted as it's possible to be, is
connected by blood to people in three continents, one of
whom was about to descend on him for a week.

The mistake that people like Arvind make is to think
their condition unique. This in turn becomes a strategy
for survival: I don't belong to a specific corner of the
earth I can call my own, he tells himself, but at least I
possess a distinctive destiny. He is encouraged to think

in this way, to see himself as some kind of freak, by those who imagine they have escaped his dilemma; and in no time at all he has become a scapegoat to be pitied or repatriated, according to your point of view. But the need for such scapegoats is itself a neurotic response to the half-glimpsed suspicion of one's own possible disintegration. The end result in either case is unhelpful, and what should properly be seen as an urgent problem of concern to every one of us has only been evaded.

When Ray Honeyford is perturbed by the 'hysterical' Sikh at the school meeting he fails to see that he has merely identified his own complimentary hysteria. Both men are feeding off each other; both seek to preserve tradition – the Koran, Wordsworth – in the face of their Terror (à la Roy Kerridge) at a world turned upside-down. Their similarities in this regard are greater than their differences, colour, religion and country of birth notwithstanding. Unfortunately, the object of all this hysteria – the Sikh's child, Honeyford's pupil – is overlooked in the barrage of insults traded across a school hall. Yet it is the child, caught in the crossfire, whose condition is the most attenuated of all.

But I want to say to that child that he and his family *are* British; I want to say that it's right and proper for them to assert their Britishness and be proud of it, whatever they are otherwise told by those who would seek to deny them something so fundamental that the very attempt to do so makes one incredulous. And I want to say to those who define culture and belonging so narrowly as to exclude this child, that cultures are not monolithic entities fixed for ever in a timeless universe, but that the measure of a culture is its ability to confront and assimilate the challenge of new visions. I want to say that when we have at last opened our eyes and learnt to properly see every child born here as a British child, we might also see the variety and the richness that is our heritage, and our salvation.

I want to say these things because they need to be said without qualification; and if I'm able to say them it's because my grandparents, who couldn't tell me how to deal with being called a 'wog' in the school playground, nevertheless could tell me, in ways they never knew, that I very much belonged, and that my sense of belonging had little or nothing to do with a word carelessly used. And what better tribute could I pay them than make a pilgrimage to the small village in the Scottish Highlands from which, at the turn of the century, my grandfather had begun his own journey?

England began to fall away even before I crossed the border with Scotland. The small, overcrowded island, in which one town led almost directly into the next, became the open spaces of Northumberland. I called in, briefly, on a couple I had known in Ireland. Their farmhouse was easy to spot by the brightly coloured teepee that stood beside it. They had since added four more children to the ten they had when we knew them. Steve muttered something about astrological birth-control as he emptied a catering size can of baked beans into a huge pot on the range.

Jane yelled at the children crowding her at the table. She looked exhausted, as well she might. I asked them how they liked living in Britain. They had seemed so rooted in Ireland, so much part of the temper of the place, that I was surprised when I heard they were leaving. Steve said, 'I think of money all the time; I'm sick of this poverty.' He motioned towards the children. So it had all been a mistake. The hippy dream of children and living in the country had become hard work and denial. Jane said, 'I'll be over sixty when this one leaves home,' and she indicated the baby at her breast.

They gave me the address of a friend of theirs in Edinburgh. When I crossed the border and saw the sign welcoming me to Scotland I felt a slight rush in my stomach. It wasn't my first visit to Scotland, but the nature of this journey made it a homecoming of sorts. This was my grandfather's country and therefore mine also. I belonged here; Scotland was my birthright.

I called at the address I had been given by Steve. The woman who answered the door didn't say very much when I introduced myself. We went through to the kitchen. Over the fireplace there was a framed motto with the single word: BE. This clearly translated as: we don't have to talk in order to relax in each other's company. She hardly spoke to me at all, but I wasn't laid-back enough to feel entirely comfortable with the silence. For all I knew I may have been an imposition she didn't want, and that she was perhaps only tolerating me out of a notion of duty. It turned out that she was a member of the Hare Krishna sect, as I discovered from the postcard on the mantelpiece in the front room where I slept:

Dear –
Haribal! Thank you for your letter. Glad *mine* made some sense! I didn't neglect any of my duties to write – that *is* my duty! I very much like your idea of devotees on the 'soaps' – we just seem to pop up in comedy shows so far! Please say Haribal to Renu if you see her.
Hare Krishna,
Kripamoya dasa

145

The silence eventually drove me out for the evening, but Edinburgh is such a majestic city that I didn't mind at all. It was also a city built for walking; and as I headed for the city centre I caught myself fantasising about living here and learning Gaelic and walking down Princes Street in a kilt.

There was a hint of frost on the ground when I set off the next morning. I kept to the coast road as far as Aberdeen, where Paul Theroux, in the course of his own journey, almost got into a fight with a bouncer who wouldn't let him into a country and western club because he was wearing jeans:

'Ye canna wear blue jeans here. Regulations.'
'Are you serious? I can't wear blue jeans to an evening of country and western music?'
'Ye canna.'
I said, 'How do you know I'm not Willie Nelson?'
He jabbed me hard with his stubby finger and said, 'You're nae Wullie Nullson, now piss off!'

Theroux didn't like Aberdeen, but I found the city friendly enough. I booked into a hotel, a rare luxury given my resources, and went for a walk around the docks. A Russian ship had docked earlier in the day, and drunken Russian voices poured out of the sleazy-looking bars while the hookers stood on the corner watching the cars cruise by on the cobbled streets.

The next morning I cut across to Inverness and then into the Highlands. I hadn't imagined that the scenery would be so breath-taking. Majestic was the word that kept coming to my mind: Scotland is majestic where

England is cosy and Wales is rugged. I drove on and on and on, the mountains giving way to lochs and then mountains again.

I spent the night in Thurso, a pretty little town on the northern coast. I noticed a Chinese take-away, and I wondered how they had managed to come so far. It's unusual for immigrants to stray so far from the anonymity and safety of the cities. Before I turned in for the night I went and stood on the shore. I could get a boat from here and head north until I reached the Arctic. Less ambitiously, I thought that I might catch a ferry to the Orkney Islands, but in the morning I just kept driving.

I stopped at Dounreay because they were advertising tours that day and it was such a splendid name for an experimental nuclear reactor. Dounreay, Doomreay: only civil servants would overlook the suggestion of death and darkness. I stopped again in Ullapool, where I had my first proper haggis. I had eaten haggis before, but it was out of a tin. I had liked it then but I liked it even better now, and I took this to be proof of my indisputable Scottishness.

It was late when I reached Fort William and I decided to spend the night there. I was still a fair distance from Acharacle and I knew I would have difficulty finding the place in the dark. In the morning I set off towards Mallaig. I left the main road at Lochailort and followed the single-track lane. I almost went through the village before I realised that I had finally arrived at my destination. I parked the car and lit a cigarette and looked down at Loch Shiel. It was as stunning as my mother said it would be when I first told her of my journey.

There was a cemetery nearby. I went in and hunted around for my grandparents' headstone. I had trouble finding it among the Camerons who had been buried there over the years, including perhaps one Captain Cameron who accompanied the author James Hogg not far from here during his tour of the Highlands in 1803. And then I saw it:

IN MEMORY OF
DONALD CAMERON
AND HIS WIFE ELLA.
REST IN PEACE.

I sat on the grass beside the headstone and turned my face to the sun and I thought down through the years. I recalled how it was when I first lived with them in Streatham: meeting my grandfather on the corner after school; going to the shops with my grandmother on Saturday morning; getting on and off buses on our way to the Tower. And I remembered the night I left for Lagos eighteen months later. I remember my grandmother weeping into her handkerchief and my grandfather with his arm around her, the pair of them watching me go through immigration control and perhaps hoping for a miracle which would suddenly make everything all right and we'd be back at home in front of the fire, my grandmother with her knitting on her lap, my grandfather pulling on his pipe. There was no chance of that. My mother had already gone ahead of me a fortnight before.

It was five years before I saw them again. In all that time I thought about nothing but coming back. One day I ran away from home thinking I could make it to Britain but I allowed the friend of my mother whom I had gone to see, an Englishwoman married to a

148

Nigerian doctor, to persuade me to let her call my father and tell him I was safe. All the same she was worried and she wrote my mother.

When I finally made it back Britain had become a mythical place of order and tranquillity. This wasn't difficult against the background of military coups and a civil war in Nigeria which only reflected the upheavals in my father's house, and my own sense of emotional confusion and unhappiness. My image of Britain may for this reason even now be distorted – it is still an ordered and tranquil country – but all visions are in any case partial; any vision of a country can only ever be the truth of one person's experience.

The Britain to which I returned at sixteen couldn't be the same as the Britain I had left as an eleven-year-old; it couldn't be the Britain of an eleven-year-old's imagination even if it still represented a haven of sorts to the sixteen-year-old. My grandparents didn't understand this; they didn't even understand – but how could they? – that all this coming and going, apparently so effortless – eight hours in a plane, no more – was emotionally disastrous. Human beings aren't designed to cope with such violent change; we aren't programmed to wake up one morning in the heat and humidity and the red earth of Lagos and go to bed the same evening in a freezing London attic room, the snow falling gently on the windowpane outside.

I was fractured. I had to make myself all over again but I didn't know how to go about it. I didn't even know what it was that I had to do. And nobody could tell me, not even my grandparents. It was outside the range of their experience; and although I didn't live with them as before in the house in Streatham which had once meant so much to me, the house with the road leading to the common and the memory of Sunday afternoons by the fire, they were hurt that I didn't visit them as often as they had every right to expect.

When I did go and see them I was casual, off-hand, perhaps because I needed to protect myself against the conflicting emotional demands with which I was having to cope, perhaps because I was simply disoriented: every night for the first three months, as I prepared for sleep, I had the terrifying sensation that I was looking down on myself from a great height. The moment I switched off the light I would feel myself leaving my body and ascending to the corner of the room where two walls met until I was two eyes and a consciousness watching the body on the bed so that I delayed the darkness until the end of the next chapter, and the next, and the next . . .

This was my first intimation of death, the terrible knowledge that we are born to die and that there is no reprieve, no possibility of a second chance. And I knew, then, that our connection to this gift of life is extraordinarily fragile. If somebody had suddenly called my name during these out-of-body experiences I wouldn't have been able to get back in time. I didn't talk about this to anybody, least of all my grandparents. It would have disturbed them and made them fearful for me and they would have pretended to dismiss it as they had once dismissed the name-calling at school. It was better for me to remain silent. But this meant that I had begun a secret life apart from them at a time when I lacked the maturity to explore a new kind of relationship. The resulting tension came between us, and I let it show.

One day, shortly after I had gone up to university, they made a two-hundred-mile detour just to visit me. They were on their way back from Scotland to their retirement cottage in Cornwall. They were already elderly then and the extra journey must have taken considerable effort on their part. They booked into a bed-and-breakfast overlooking the sea on the Mumbles, a few miles out of central Swansea, and invited me over for tea. When I arrived my grandmother unpacked the delicate bone-china cups and saucers and the matching plates she always took with her on holiday. Crass and ungrateful as I was, I let my irritation show and left as soon as I could. Not long afterwards they died.

We expected my grandfather to die first. He was eighty-seven and had cancer of the spine and there was nothing to be done. I went with my mother to see them, the train curving round the Cornish coast as the sun rose across the sea on a beautiful autumn morning. We were met at the station by my grandmother, who promptly burst into tears when she saw us. 'I don't know what I'll do when he's gone,' she said, and I gathered that the doctor had just been to see him.

In the event it was my grandmother who died first, shortly before I left for Ireland. It was at her funeral that I met Don, my grandfather's nephew, my second cousin. He and a friend had driven all the way down from Acharacle just for the funeral, a display of family obligation I wouldn't have found surprising in Nigeria but which struck me as unusual in what I had come to know of Britain. Don and I and his friend and another man were pall-bearers. The service was held in one of those small country churches on a beautiful late-September afternoon. The light streamed through the stained-glass windows and when I looked over at my grandfather, who had already prepared himself for his own death, I was pleased that I was at least able to make some amends for the shoddy way I had treated them. I stayed on for a few days after the funeral. I helped him wash, dress, climb the stairs. A week after I left for Ireland my mother wrote to say that he was dead.

But why had my grandfather left his village in the

first place? Don, when we spoke later, put it down to simple ambition. My grandfather wanted to get on; he wanted to make something of his life. Certainly there wouldn't have been much to keep an ambitious man in those days; and even Don, who is of my mother's generation, recalls levels of poverty in his childhood that I have only ever heard described in Ireland.

This was in keeping with what I already knew of the Celtic experience. It seems that the Celts have always been penalised when things get rough, as I had already witnessed in the Welsh valleys in the mid-1970s. I have rarely encountered scenes as desolate as a Welsh mining village in the perpetual drizzle of the valleys: the smoke hanging in the air above the houses; the despair on the faces of the unemployed men; the women picking their way through the puddles in thin, cheap shoes to the corner shop; the pallid features of the children fed on a diet of sugar and starch.

It's possible that this is what my grandfather saw when he decided to leave; but if Don was right and ambition alone had driven my grandfather away, why hadn't the others left? Of the entire family only he had escaped. The others continued to live there, some even in the very cottages in which they had been born at the turn of the century, so many great-uncles and great-aunts who all welcomed me with strong whisky and dim memories of the man I had come to honour as I visited each of them in turn over the next few days. My grandfather was deeply loved, and yet he had left with probably no more thought for the journey he was undertaking than I gave to my own flight from Nigeria. But the price only comes later, the thoughts of loss and the feelings of grief that can tear you apart at the sudden recollection of a smell or a sound or a voice.

My answer, perhaps unsatisfactory, was that he had

been driven to leave out of an obscure necessity. The consequences of my grandfather's flight were far-reaching, and must have caused him great sadness in old age: all three of his children married foreigners and went to live abroad. It was as if, by upsetting the delicate balance of the continuity of place that day he walked down the lane and across the fields and along the side of the loch that led to Fort William – maybe even at this time of the year – and caught the train to Glasgow, he brought in its wake a profound dislocation in the succeeding generations, like the ripples on the loch overlooking the site of the ruined croft in which he was born. I have cousins who emigrated to America, Canada, Jamaica; those of us who continue to live in Britain do so with the presence of another culture as a profound part of our complex inheritance.

My grandfather anticipated the modern world, the great movement of peoples across continents which has only recently come to an end. If our century is distinctive it isn't only because of our impressive technology but this intermingling of cultures on the grand scale. For reasons of empire Britain has been forced to confront the meaning of the modern migration more immediately than most other societies. The Scots played a disproportionately large part in the imperial adventure, but mostly as explorers and missionaries and engineers rather than administrators. It may even have been the Scottish sense of defeat at the hands of the Sassenachs which drove them to the furthest corners; and perhaps my grandfather's own journey expressed the working-out of the terrible restlessness that comes with defeat.

But in my grandfather's case there was an added poignancy about his journey which was thrown into relief during my stay at Acharacle. What had his journey amounted to? A trench in France and a job in the

Post Office? This was hardly a success story. Don, who had stayed, was a successful businessman with his own building firm and a brand-new three-bedroom bungalow overlooking the loch in which my grandfather had fished for trout whenever he was able to return.

Did my grandfather's journey amount to nothing? This was the question I turned over and over in my mind when I returned again to the cemetery the day before I left. It was dusk, a melancholy time of day. The light from the dying sun filtered through the golden-brown leaves and I thought how much this man had meant to me, how much his memory would continue to mean to me. And I knew that I had at least paid him the only tribute that I could by undertaking the journey to the village of his birth, and that in doing so something had been completed.